IRISH UNIVERSITY STUDENTS WITH MENTAL HEALTH DIFFICULTIES

Emma Farrell

IRISH UNIVERSITY STUDENTS WITH MENTAL HEALTH DIFFICULTIES

Experiences, Challenges, and Supports

The Education Studies Collection

Collection Editor

Janise Hurtig

First published in 2024 by Lived Places Publishing

All rights reserved. No part of this publication may be reproduced, stored in a retrieval system, or transmitted in any form or by any means, electronic, mechanical, photocopying, recording or otherwise, without prior permission in writing from the publisher.

The author and editors have made every effort to ensure the accuracy of information contained in this publication, but assume no responsibility for any errors, inaccuracies, inconsistencies, and omissions. Likewise, every effort has been made to contact copyright holders. If any copyright material has been reproduced unwittingly and without permission the Publisher will gladly receive information enabling them to rectify any error or omission in subsequent editions.

Copyright © 2024 Emma Farrell

British Library Cataloguing in Publication Data
A CIP record for this book is available from the British Library

ISBN: 9781916704855 (pbk)
ISBN: 9781916704879 (ePDF)
ISBN: 9781916704862 (ePUB)

The right of Emma Farrell to be identified as the Author of this work have been asserted by them in accordance with the Copyright, Design and Patents Act 1988.

Cover design by Fiachra McCarthy
Book design by Rachel Trolove of Twin Trail Design
Typeset by Newgen Publishing UK

Lived Places Publishing
Long Island
New York 11789

www.livedplacespublishing.com

Abstract

This book explores the nature and meaning of higher education for Irish university students with mental health difficulties. It does this by understanding the lived experience of these students. Understanding lived experience is one of the most powerful, yet under-appreciated, forms of knowledge available. This book illuminates the value of lived experience in informing inclusive education policy and practice. It offers an understanding of the experiences of students, their routes to higher education, the challenges they face, and their experiences of the supports that are available to them. It offers valuable insights and reflections on the nature and meaning of higher education for students in distress and the efforts these students invest in managing their mental health so that they may complete their university education. The book aims to provide insight and understanding for educators, student support providers, and students on professional courses so that they may better support students struggling with their mental health while at university.

Keywords

Mental health; well-being; university; education; mental illness; lived experience; students; disability; policy

Acknowledgements

I am extremely grateful to all those whose influence is represented, if only indirectly, in the pages of this book. It represents many years of research and conversations with thoughtful and thought-provoking colleagues and friends. I would particularly like to thank Dara Ryder CEO of AHEAD – the Association for Higher Education Access and Disability – for his consultative input and support.

This book is dedicated to the students who shared their experiences and to Professor Michael Shevlin in appreciation of his commitment to supporting brave and original research and practice in inclusive education.

Contents

Chapter 1	Introduction	1
	Learning objectives	1
Chapter 2	The Irish context	9
	Learning objectives	9
Chapter 3	Transition to higher education	25
	Learning objectives	25
Chapter 4	Disability support	39
	Learning objectives	39
Chapter 5	The lived experience of navigating higher education with a mental health difficulty	55
	Learning objectives	55
Chapter 6	Analysis, implications, and reflections	85
	Learning objectives	85
Appendix		98
Recommended assignments		133
Notes		137
References		138
Index		155

1
Introduction

Learning objectives

1. **To become familiar with the many ways of knowing** and the importance of understanding lived experience.
2. **To develop an understanding of the factors shaping the changing terminology for distress** and the socio-political factors shaping these changes.

In 2021/22, the non-progression rate [in Irish higher education] was 15%, representing an increase of 3 percentage points.
Students with a disability are less likely to progress [than students without a disability] but more so if they have a psychological or mental health condition.

(Higher Education Authority, 2024c)

I got very ill in first year in college, [it] just went terribly, I did the wrong course which didn't help. I didn't really meet people that I clicked with and I'd kind of been putting a lot of hope on that in college. I lived with my boyfriend at the time and another couple, and one of my flatmates who we think might have had some social issues but he was very particular and he just made the house a nightmare, and my relationship started to fall apart and everything got terrible and I ended up just not going to college from January onwards. I pretty much got very depressed, very anxious. I got very, very anxious. It was very, very, very bad. Yeah, so that went on for a few months kind of and by the time I got home that June I was just, I kind of collapsed, I was so tired and I don't think I've ever been so exhausted, so mentally exhausted in my life as I was that year.

(Ella)

As soon as I started college my mental health fell apart. I was really depressed, really anxious, couldn't function here in college, I was overwhelmed. My shakes were back, I wasn't able to control my thoughts and the words would come into my head "I'm not intelligent", "I'm not meant to be here", "how did I get in here". Suicide kept crossing my mind and it came to a point where I wasn't able to do my work.

(John)

The quotes above from Ella and John, both names self-chosen pseudonyms, add meaning to the Higher Education Authority's statistics. They help us to move beyond percentage points or trends, important as these are, and into the minds, thoughts, feelings, and experiences of students who, in Ella's case at least, are represented in these non-progression statistics. Ella and John's stories open up our understanding of the experience of drop-out and the array of utterly understandable factors that result in non-progression. Factors, that upon learning them, we too can imagine how, if faced with such difficult thoughts, feelings and experiences, we might have followed a similar path. Their stories allow us to learn, not only with our minds but with our spirits, the meaning of experiences. In short, they allow us to understand. As Munhall suggests, "isn't that what we all wish for – to be understood?" (Munhall, 1994, p. 170).

This book is all about understanding. Its aim is to offer an insight into the lived experience of Irish university students with mental health difficulties so that readers might better be able to say "I understand". It offers an understanding of the experiences of students, their routes to higher education, the barriers they face, and the assumptions underpinning their presence on campus. It offers valuable insights into diagnosis, support, and the efforts students invest in managing their mental health so that they may complete their university education. This chapter sets the scene for understanding. It examines how we understand, the words with which we create and name this understanding, and why understanding is important in the first place. In doing so, this chapter lays important groundwork for the insights to come. It begins with a description of why I wrote this book and, in particular, sought to focus on understanding rather than describing or explaining. From here on I, as author and researcher, take a step back and allow the lived experiences themselves to come to the fore. The chapter concludes with consideration of the terminology that will be used throughout to refer to a phenomenon that can variously be described as illness, disorder, or distress.

Researching lived experience

As an undergraduate student I learned that one in four adults will experience a mental health difficulty at any one point in time (Ginn and Horder, 2012). I read studies that suggested that

75 per cent of adults with a mental health difficulty can trace its origin back to between the ages of 18 and 25 (Kessler et al., 2005) – a time when many young people are engaged in higher education. I was taught to statistically analyse a whole host of psychological phenomena – from anxiety to resilience – using a range of sophisticated measures and techniques, and look with confidence to the score at the end of the measure for insight. Yet, beyond my studies I had the privilege of listening to the rich and deeply nuanced stories of young people with lived experience of distress. Through my work as a founding member of Jigsaw, Ireland's National Centre for Youth Mental Health, I had the privilege of bearing witness to stories of fear, hurt, shame, and disappointment. I learned how distress manifests and grows in climates of poverty, unrelenting competition and expectations, loneliness, and/or neglect. I heard stories of hopelessness and strength; despair and indomitable courage; desperation and wisdom, that offered insight, depth, clarity, and understanding. Yet, I found little more than snippets of these in the academic papers and textbooks that filled the university library.

I realised that we live in a society that prizes the "self-correcting features of modern science" (US Department of Health and Human Services, 2001) over the "swampy lowlands of human experience" (Barker, Campbell and Davidson, 1999). Stories and lived experiences are all too often posited as "strictly speaking, not science" (Jensen and Redman, 2024) and therefore, not valuable. However, stories, for me, are immensely valuable. They offer a path to understanding that we forsake for the twin illusions of certainty and objectivity. Objectivity is a subjective concept and good science relies on a range of perspectives from a diverse community (Oreskes, 2021). It requires both science and stories.

This is particularly true of mental health where, for too long, the voices of those with lived experience have been disregarded, even considered unreliable, unavailing, and untrustworthy. This has resulted in significant epistemic injustice where the testimony and interpretations of people with lived experience of distress is considered lacking in credibility, and they are actively undermined in their capacity as knowers and contributors to their own diagnosis and response (Crichton, Carel, and Kidd, 2017). Instead, as Chapter 2 will explore, we have relied heavily in recent decades, on a medico-scientific approach to distress. Trying to understand the complexity of human distress from this medico-scientific perspective alone is, as Boss suggests, akin to trying to understand a Picasso painting in terms of "material objects whose length and breadth could be measured, whose weight could be determined, and whose substance could be analysed chemically" (Boss, 1979, p. 100). These data "would tell us nothing about what makes these paintings what they are, their character as works of art is not even touched" (Boss, 1979, p. 100). This approach, as a group of 29 psychiatrists (Bracken et al., 2012, p. 432) put it, "has not served psychiatry well". Instead they call for greater emphasis on understanding and honouring lived experience in mental health.

> Good psychiatry involves active engagement with the complex nature of mental health problems, a healthy scepticism for biological reductionism, tolerance for the tangled nature of relationships and meanings, and the

> ability to negotiate these issues in a way that empowers service users and their carers.
>
> (Bracken et al., 2012, p. 432)

My aspiration in conducting the research that forms the basis of this book was to neither explain nor analyse but rather to understand. It was to reinstate the value of understanding by demonstrating, not just its transformative potential, but its trustworthiness (see Appendix) as a form of knowledge upon which to build policy and practice. Following Bracken and colleagues above, this research sought to actively engage with the complex nature of mental health and distress. It sought to honour people's lived experiences as a valuable, indeed essential, form of knowledge. More specifically, I sought to understand the nature and meaning of higher education for students with mental health difficulties.

A note on terminology

> Silence is the language of God,
> all else is poor translation.
>
> (Rumi)

The language adopted to convey the phenomenon of distress has evolved throughout history in line with popular conceptualisations. From "lunacy" (reflecting early beliefs about the pernicious influences of the moon) to "melancholia" ("black bile"); from madness (the word "mad" introduced to replace the Old English word "wod" which means demonically possessed or frenzied) to mental illness; the choice and appropriateness of language related to distress depends more on the dominant perspective of the time than the experience itself.

The last 60 years alone have seen a largely interchangeable array of terms from mental illness which, following a 1960s critique of the biological basis for distress (Foucault, 1961; Goffman, 1961; 1963; Laing, 1960; Szasz, 1960), gave way to disorder, which by the early twenty-first century had itself given way to terms such as "mental health problem" or "mental health condition". This alteration in terminology is seen in Ireland's mental health policy – from the 1984 policy which catered for the "mentally ill" (Department of Health and Children, 1984) to the 2006 policy which primarily focused on people with "mental health problems" (Department of Health and Children, 2006) to the 2020 policy which further differentiates those with a "mental health difficulty" and those with "severe mental disorders" (Department of Health, 2020). However, as Beresford (2005) and others would argue, the replacement of terms such as "mental illness" and "pathology" with the more euphemistic "mental health" or "mental health difficulties" does little to change their origins, meanings, and legal basis. The term mental illness, in its true or euphemistic form, clearly suggests an understanding of these matters as related to health and sickness. These experiences, as explored in Chapter 2, will be predisposed to a medical interpretation.

This book, in line with the principles of hermeneutic phenomenology (described in Appendix), seeks to remain open to the phenomenon. As such, it aspires to avoid familiar terminology and assumptions of illness or disorder and remain as close to the phenomenon as it is lived as possible. Accordingly, the term distress will be used in this book to describe experiences that others might describe as mental illness or mental health difficulties. The one thing most people can agree on in relation to these experiences is that they can be distressing. The term distress will be interchanged with "mental health difficulty", "mental health", or "mental distress", if only for variety. Where possible or appropriate, the students' own choice of terminology will always take precedence. Interestingly, the most commonly used term by those who shared their experiences of distress was simply "it". This term will be used, both in respect for the student's own conceptualisation and in recognition that "it" is a uniquely personal experience perhaps beyond explanation, generalisation, and definition on a grand scale.

The term "university" will be used to refer to all Higher Education Institutions (HEIs) funded by Ireland's Department of Further and Higher Education, Research, Innovation and Science (DFHERIS) via the Higher Education Authority. These include universities, technological universities, and other institutions that receive public funding. Students who participated in this research came from across the higher education sector, with the majority attending any one of Ireland's seven universities.

2
The Irish context

Learning objectives

1. **To become familiar with the history of mental health in Ireland** and develop a critical understanding of the dominance of the illness framework of distress.
2. **To understand the impact of widening participation and concurrent decreased funding** on universities' ability to respond to the needs of an increasingly diverse student population.
3. **To critically analyse the current model of support for students with mental health difficulties in higher education** and interrogate the effectiveness and equity of this approach.

Introduction

Sixty years ago this book would not have been necessary. Higher education was the preserve of a small minority, and those struggling with their mental health would likely have been housed in institutions, homeless, or hidden away. Since the 1960s, participation in higher education has grown 13-fold – from 18,427 students in 1964 to 246,300 students in 2021; our response to mental health has shifted from one of incarceration to inclusion; and there is a greater public awareness of mental health and well-being than ever before. This chapter charts these developments. It explores the history of our response to distress, the rapid growth of the higher education sector in Ireland, and the implications of consecutive policies of increased participation and decreased investment in higher education for students with mental health difficulties. Finally, this chapter engages with the "why" and "how" of universities' support for students with mental health difficulties and asks if the current approach is achieving its stated aim of facilitating a more equitable engagement with higher education for students in distress.

Mental health in Ireland: A brief history

The history of mental health in Ireland, like that of so many western nations, charts an unfolding array of words, descriptions, understandings, and approaches to the phenomenon that today we variously describe as difficulty, distress, or disorder. Our earliest ancestors understood madness as a form of supernatural retribution. One of the most dreaded necromantic powers of the Irish druids was that of causing madness. For this purpose and angry druids would prepare a "madman's wisp" (dluí fulla), a ball of straw or grass, which he cursed and flung into the face of his victim who at once became insane or idiotic (Kelly, 2016; Robins, 1986). Little distinction was drawn at that time between those described as "mad" and those who today would be referred to as having an intellectual disability.

The arrival of Christianity to Ireland did little to alter prevailing supernatural or pagan beliefs but merely, as Robins (1986, p. 4) puts it, "put a Christian gloss on existing notions". This gloss painted insanity as the wrath of God as opposed to retribution from the intermediaries of the pagan otherworld. The belief in demoniacal possession, both in its older pagan and newer Christian forms, captured the imagination of the medieval mind. The world and its inhabitants were seen as the chief prizes in a constant battle between good and evil, light and darkness, God and Satan (Deutsch, 1937). Throughout Europe people, particularly women whose mental aberrance or abnormal behaviour failed to meet the Church's and society's rigidly ordained beliefs and practices, were accused of being witches, cruelly tortured, and put to death. This was particularly the case in Protestant countries where the sixteenth-century Protestant reformation had spurred what Robins (1986, p. 19) refers to as an "orgy of witch-hunting". Throughout Europe tens of thousands of alleged witches were put to death, "many of them were insane persons" (Robins, 1986, p. 18).

Celtic Ireland largely escaped this frenzy of witch-hunting and instead adopted a more inclusive and pragmatic approach to managing "the mad". The Brehon Laws, ancient statutes that governed pre-Christian and early Christian Ireland, outlined considerable provisions for the inclusion and protection of the insane (Kelly, 2005). For example, the Seanchas Mór, or "Law of Distress", dictated that failing to support or provide maintenance for a family member resulted in a fine; five cows for failing to maintain a madman and ten cows for failing to maintain a madwoman, considerable fines at that time reflecting the unequal resources available to men and women. However, since the Brehon Laws focused on protection from abuse rather than neglect, life for the "mad" in the Middle Ages and Early Modern Ireland tended to be harsh and impoverished (Kelly, 2016). These harsh conditions were further compounded when, following increased control by, and eventual union with, Great Britain, Irish monasteries, and their monastic hospitals, were dissolved. This led to even greater levels of homeless, neglect, and incarceration (Finnane, 1981; Robins, 1986).

> Little distinction was drawn between them. The beggar, the prostitute, the cripple, the scrofulous, the runaway apprentice, the imbecile and the mad were locked up in a variety of penal institutions where all were treated with great harshness.
>
> (Robins, 1986, p. 24)

By the late eighteenth century, growing concerns over abuses and conditions in Irish jails led to the establishment of Houses of Industry at Dublin, Clonmel, Cork, Waterford, and Limerick. These houses were punitive rather than charitable in design and sought to confine and control "sturdy beggars and vagabonds" as well as give some shelter to the "deserving poor" (Walsh and Daly, 2004, p. 14). The proportion of insane in these Houses of Industry grew to such an extent that, by 1810, a grant was provided to the Dublin House of Industry to establish an asylum "for the reception of lunatics from all parts of the kingdom" (Kirkpatrick, 1931, p. 17). This asylum, the Richmond Asylum, was filled to capacity within two years of its opening and led the British Government to launch an expansion of the asylum system that, by 1900, resulted in 22 public asylums throughout the country housing 17,000 inmates – 56 for every 10,000 Irish citizens (compared with 41 in England and Wales and 45 in Scotland (Inspectors of Lunatics, 1901; 1906). Medical doctors "were put in charge of asylums primarily because they were easy to hold accountable to the board of governors" (Burns, 2006, p. 37). In the absence of effective medical interventions the superintendent's role was predominately administrative and disciplinary. In the 1840s superintendents began to found their own professional bodies and "the previously heterogeneous congeries of madhouse keepers had instead become a more and more organised group of specialists" (Scull, 2011, p. 50). The new profession struggled to reach international consensus on what it should be called: the French preferred "aliéniste", the Germans "Psychiater", while their English-speaking counterparts favoured "Medical Psychologist" or "Asylum Superintendent". Ultimately, as a result of the early advancements of German physicians, the budding profession became known as psychiatry.

The development of psychiatry was supported and nourished by a variety of sociocultural conditions. First, at a basic level, physicians provided a useful service to the families and communities, "meeting the complex needs of troubled families (often unrelated to mental illness)" (Kelly, 2023, p. xvi). Second, their presence painted "a medical gloss" (Scull, 2011, p. 58) on the asylum system, a gloss that, in the wake of a series of significant medical advancements such as Pasteur and Koch's breakthroughs in medical microbiology, generated much social approval. Third, a new concept of "degeneration", which viewed the insane as "degenerate human beings" (Morel, 1857, p. 5), became increasingly popular in the era of Social Darwinism and resulted in the source of madness being firmly (re)located in the physical body. Finally, supporting the increasingly popular opinion that "patients with so-called 'mental illnesses' are really individuals with diseases of the nerves and the brain" (Griesenger, 1867, p. 1) was the discovery in 1906 by German psychiatrist Alois Alzheimer of brain anomalies associated with the disease that was named after him. This, combined with the discovery of an organic source of syphilis-induced psychosis, bolstered psychiatry's explanation of mental disorder.

While the results of German laboratory-based brain research were impressive and placed psychiatry in the same realm as other biomedical disciplines, these advancements failed to make "any contribution whatsoever to clinical care, let alone cure" (Scull, 1979, p. 68). If anything, they only served to generate a very heavily pessimistic view of the long-term prospects of those in distress. The growth of large asylums also provided captive populations for those psychiatrists who wished to conduct research. Indeed, Professor Brendan Kelly, in his seminal history of psychiatry in Ireland, describes the history of psychiatry as "a history of therapeutic enthusiasm" (2016, p. 1). Insulin-induced comas, electricity-induced seizures, malarial mosquitoes (whose use in the treatment of psychosis resulted in its pioneer receiving a Nobel Prize in 1927), and prefrontal lobotomy (which too won a Nobel Prize in 1949) were all well intentioned but ultimately barbarous attempts to root out the biological cause of distress.

> The illness framework is the dominant framework in mental health services because psychiatry is the dominant profession within those services. However, its dominance should not be confused with its conceptual superiority.
>
> (Rogers and Pilgrim, 2014, p. 2)

The illness framework, as we will see in the next section, is not just the dominant framework in mental health services but also underpins the provision of support for students with mental health difficulties in higher education. This framework seeks to identify sick individuals (diagnosis), predict the future course of their illness (prognosis), speculate about its cause (aetiology), and prescribe a response to the illness to cure or ameliorate its symptoms (treatment). The difficulty with applying an illness framework to mental health is, as the introductory chapters to the *Oxford Handbook of Psychiatry* (Semple and Smyth, 2013, p. 30) attests, (a) there are "no objective diagnostic or prognostic investigations" for mental illness (diagnosis); (b) psychiatrists "lack knowledge of the aetiology and pathogensis of most psychiatric disorders" (aetiology); and (c) the treatments or interventions are "often minimally or only partially effective" (treatment).

The dominance of the illness framework, or biomedical model, of distress has been repeatedly called into question by sociologists (Coppock and Hopton, 2000; Goffman, 1961; 1963; Horowitz, 2020; Rogers and Pilgrim, 2014; Rose, 1998; 2006; 2019), psychologists (Cromby, Harper and Reavey, 2013; Hornstein, 2017; Johnstone, 2000; Johnstone et al., 2018; Watson, 2019; Watts, 2017), psychiatrists (Bracken, 2015; Bracken and Thomas, 2001; Kleinman, 1991; 2012; Laing, 1960; Moncrieff, 2007; 2013; Szasz, 1961), philosophers (Bracken and Thomas, 2005; Foucault, 2001; 2006) and those with lived experience (Dillon, 2011; Dillon and Hornstein, 2013; Rose, 2017; Watts, 2012). The role of trauma, adverse childhood experiences, power, inequity, and discrimination, in their many complex and nefarious forms, is increasingly recognised as critical to our understanding of, and response to, human difficulty or distress (Felitti et al., 1998; Johnstone et al., 2018; Maté and Maté, 2022; Van der Kolk, 2014). However, in spite of increasing recognition of its limitations, Ireland's Higher Education Authority (HEA) continues to rely on the illness framework as the basis for the delineation of "deserving and non-deserving", to borrow the popular phrase from nineteenth-century social policy, students in their allocation of scare resources (Farrell, 2022a; Farrell and Mahon, 2021).

Higher education in Ireland

Education has always been highly valued in Ireland. Even in times of great political, social, and economic difficulty, when harsh penal legislation denied Irish Catholics (who represented the majority of the population) access to education, there was in existence a vast network of illegal "hedge schools" which catered for the majority of the Irish school-going population (Raftery, 2011). During the seventeenth and eighteenth centuries, the prevailing political and social climate meant that many Irish people had to travel abroad to access higher education – drawing on the Irish colleges network and a rich tapestry of scholarly diaspora. When access was provided to state-funded primary (1831) and secondary (1966) education, Irish people were quick to utilise and take advantage of these opportunities.

The 1960s was a transformative decade in the history of Irish education, one in which the economic and societal imperative of education drove a new policy agenda. The numbers accessing third level education soared, from 18,427 in 1964 (Clancy,

1996) to 246,300 in 2021 (Institute of Public Administration, 2024). The introduction of the "Free Fees Initiative" in 1996 contributed greatly to this growth as more and more students accessed higher education, unencumbered by undergraduate tuition fees. Prior to the introduction of "free fees", 22 per cent of Irish adults had a third level qualification (Central Statistics Office, 2000). Today this figure stands at almost 50 per cent (Central Statistics Office, 2016) and looks set to rise even further as, 80 per cent of school leavers progress each year to higher education (The Irish Times, 2023). However, from the early 2000s onwards successive governments began to reintroduce a "student contribution charge" which, following the economic crash in 2008, increased to €3,000, making Ireland one of the most expensive places to go to university in the European Union (Citizens Information, 2023). The government could no longer afford to fund free higher education and, at a time when student numbers were on the rise, exchequer investment dramatically decreased. Today it is estimated that the higher education sector in Ireland is underfunded to the tune of €307 million per year (Irish Universities Association, 2023).

The consequences of this underinvestment have been felt across the higher education sector; from increased student–staff ratios, to ageing infrastructure and a reliance on international student fees and private investment to sustain the day-to-day operation of the university. It has also resulted in a scarcity of resources by which to support students with mental health difficulties in higher education and a reliance on the illness framework as the means by which these scarce resources are allocated.

Current provision for students with mental health difficulties in higher education

The number of students with mental health difficulties in higher education has risen in recent decades in line with the changing profile of students that is seen both in Ireland and internationally (Claeys-Kulik, Jørgensen, and Stöber, 2019). As the numbers attending university have risen overall, so too has the diversity and representativeness of the student cohort. The once largely homogenous student body has been replaced by non-traditional learners from diverse racial, religious, linguistic, and learning backgrounds as well as with a variety of personal circumstances and abilities. In Ireland, it is estimated that almost 40 per cent of the student body is "non-traditional" (Healy, Banks, and Ryder, 2023).

All university students in Ireland have access to some form of mental health support. This can vary widely from a specified number of free counselling sessions, to online resources and campus well-being initiatives (Higher Education Authority, 2020). For those students struggling over a longer term, or whose distress impacts their lives in more immediate ways, additional support and accommodations can be provided through the Fund for Students with Disabilities (FSD). This fund allocates resources to each HEI through the Higher Education Authority, the body with responsibility for funding and accountability in higher education. The purpose of the Fund for Students with Disabilities is to provide HEIs with funding to assist them in supporting "eligible students with disabilities so that they can participate on an equal basis with their peers" (Higher Education Authority, 2023, p. 3). Eligibility for students with a "mental health condition" (p. 15) is established by diagnosis and report from a consultant psychiatrist. Examples provided include "bipolar disorder, schizophrenia, clinical depression, severe anxiety, severe phobias, obsessive compulsive disorder, severe eating disorders and psychosis" (Higher Education Authority, 2023, p. 15).

This approach to including and supporting students with mental health difficulties in higher education is heavily predicated on the illness framework as described in the previous section. It belies a form of thinking based on Cartesian Dualism discussed in Chapter 1 that locates the "problem" in the person with little emphasis on the wider social environment and process. As McCarthy (in Quirke, Mc Guckin, and McCarthy, 2023) suggests, this implies that distress or disability is an individual problem to be fixed or accommodated so that those categorised as "disabled" (the term itself revealing the "dis"-ability) can lead a "normal" life. While initially designed so that students with discrete and medically discernible "disabilities", such as vision impairment, hearing loss, or mobility issues, might be given the support needed to access and engage with university teaching and assessment, this discernibility between "eligible" and "ineligible" (or deserving and non-deserving as described previously) students is less clear when it comes to mental health difficulties.

The number of students with mental health conditions deemed eligible for additional support has risen rapidly from 643 students in 2011/2012 (AHEAD, 2012) to 3,939 in 2021/2022 (AHEAD, 2023). The reason for this increase in unclear but is thought to include a combination of (a) growing number of students with disabilities, including mental health conditions, progressing to higher education; (b) increased public awareness of mental health conditions with more people willing to seek help with their distress; and/or (c) the increased presence of the illness framework in everyday life (Davies, 2021; Foulkes, 2021; Rose, 2006).

In a climate of increased demand, and decreased resources, the task of determining who is to be deemed "eligible" for these scarce resources is increasingly complex. This task is further complicated by the fact that mental health conditions are difficult to define. As described above, there are "no objective diagnostic or prognostic investigations" (Semple and Smyth, 2013, p. 30) by which to determine what is "normal" or "abnormal". Indeed, as the longitudinal birth cohort study, the Dunedin study, showed us, if subject to psychiatric assessment at regular intervals, 86 per cent of the general population will meet the criteria for a diagnosable mental disorder by the age of 45 (Caspi et al., 2020).

Further, more affluent students who are able to afford private psychiatric assessment, bypassing the long waiting lists and administrative delays associated with the public mental health system, are automatically advantaged in a system that relies on a psychiatric report to access services. This advantage is seen in the disproportion of students entering higher education through the DARE (Disability Access Route to Education) scheme who come from affluent backgrounds. DARE offers reduced points university places to school leavers who, as a result of having a disability, have experienced additional challenges in second level (high school) education. In effect, this means that students who come through the DARE scheme can access university places with lower "points" or grades than their peers. Data from the Higher Education Authority (2024a) reveals the 70 per cent of new entrants to university under the DARE scheme are from "marginally advantaged" or "affluent" backgrounds. Indeed, one quarter are classed as "affluent" under the deprivation index score. Given people with disabilities are known to be at higher risk of social exclusion and deprivation (Eurostat, 2022), these figures suggest that the DARE scheme is failing to represent its intended population. Indeed, anecdotal evidence suggests that the scheme is increasingly being appropriated by students, and their families, with the financial resources and know-how to pay for private assessment, diagnosis, and reports so as to access higher education through the reduced point DARE system and avail of additional supports and accommodations whilst there.

This trend is also seen in the US where a report by the *Wall Street Journal* (Belkin, Levitz, and Korn, 2019) highlighted how students from private, fee-paying schools were four times more likely to come to university with a diagnosis and thus automatically avail themselves of accommodations such as extra time in exams. Further, an ethnographic study of "mitigating circumstances" revealed a sense amongst UK university support staff that the provisions were not reaching all those for whom they are designed, but rather "the system has been co-opted by groups of vocal, confident, privileged students who know how to work the system" for personal gain (Armstrong and Byrom, 2023, p. 8). What these points serve to highlight is that the current model of support for students with mental health difficulties – indeed, it has been argued the current model of support for the entire student population (Healy, Banks, and Ryder, 2023) – is no longer fit for purpose.

In response to increased student diversity, and the recognition that the current provision of support to individual "eligible" students is neither fit for purpose nor sustainable (McCarthy, Quirke, and Treanor, 2018), there has been a shift towards a universal design for learning (UDL) approach that seeks to create more inclusive and equitable learning environments for all students – not just those identified as lacking or dis-abled in some way (Quirke, Mc Guckin, and McCarthy, 2023). Universal design for learning provides a framework for educators to proactively plan their curriculum and pedagogy so that it is more accessible to all students. It represents a shift in thinking from the university as oriented towards the "average" student, with specific measures to enable disadvantaged or disabled students "to participate on an equal basis with their peers" (Higher Education Authority, 2023, p. 3), to one that recognises the variability and individuality of all students. Research shows that by incorporating UDL into university teaching and learning many of the pressing issues associated with increasing participation and diversity in higher education – issues including student retention, performance, completion, and well-being – can be alleviated (Al-Azawei, Serenelli, and Lundqvist, 2016; Almeqdad et al., 2023; Capp, 2017; Healy, Banks, and Ryder, 2023; Soek, DaCosta, and Hodges, 2018). UDL is in its infancy in the Irish higher education context but has been received crucial support and stakeholder buy-in that has resulted in significant momentum in the introduction of UDL in Irish universities. It has been recognised and welcomed as a more inclusive and shared mode of higher education. Indeed, while there is still a distance to go before the disability model, and its reliance on the illness framework, can be consigned to history, it has been suggested that this momentum and enthusiasm positions Ireland to be a world leader in the successful implementation of UDL in higher education (Healy, Banks, and Ryder, 2023).

Conclusion

This chapter sought to set the scene by providing an overview of how Ireland has, historically, approached and responded to mental health difficulty or distress. It described the higher education sector in Ireland, charting the rapid increase in students accessing third level education since the 1960s. It aligned this rapid growth with a more recent period of austerity that has resulted in significant underfunding of Irish universities. In this climate of scarcity, a distinction is drawn between those students who are, or are not, "eligible" for additional supports or accommodations. Determining who is eligible for additional support for a "mental health condition" is, as discussed above, complex and efforts to provide a more equitable mode of support for all students have seen a turn, in recent years, towards a UDL approach to teaching and learning in higher education. The lived experience of entering the higher education context laid out in this chapter forms the focus of Chapter 3.

3
Transition to higher education

Learning objectives

1. **To understand the experience of transition to higher education for students with mental health difficulties** as one that can occur at any life stage and that can represent a gift as well as a challenge.

2. **To critically analyse the opportunities and limitations of a specialised Disability Access Route to Education (DARE) for students with mental health difficulties** and gain an awareness of the opportunities and limitations of this approach to including and supporting students with mental health difficulties.

Introduction

Starting university is a major milestone for any student. It is a time of change and a time of opportunity. While change is an inevitable, indeed beneficial, aspect of life it can also be a challenging time – particularly for those who struggle with their mental health. In this chapter the transition to higher education is explored through scholarly literature and the voices and experiences of students with lived experience of mental health difficulties. It begins by examining what is meant by transition. While often associated with young adults, transition to higher education for those who have experienced distress can occur at any life stage. This offers a helpful reminder that transitions can occur across the lifespan and the transition to higher education is not the sole domain of the transition to adulthood. Students who shared their experiences of transition to university do so at a variety of life stages and ages. These stories comprise the larger part of this chapter, with particular focus afforded to the experience of transition and the Disability Access Route to Education (DARE) by which many students have entered university.

What is a transition?

Transitions are periods in life of significant change. They are hard to avoid and most of us will have gone through a number of significant changes by the time we reach adulthood. It might be surprising, therefore, to learn that there is no agreed definition of a transition (Ecclestone et al., 2010). It has been variously described as a process and as a point in time. For example, Colley (2007, p. 428) simply describes transition as "a process of change over time" while Quinn (2009, p. 122) considers it as "a fixed turning point which takes place at a preordained time and in a certain place". Whether considered in terms of process or place, transitions are associated with changes or shifts in position, status, place, or role. Theories of human development recognise the transitions experienced by young people in their late adolescence or early 20s are more complex and multi-faceted than those experienced at other stages across the lifespan (Hutchison, 2008). Indeed, it has been suggested that the transition to higher education is "one of the most significant transitions in a student's life" (Timmis, Pexton, and Cavallerio, 2022, p. 2504). Many students leave their home communities for the first time to study in a new town or city. They leave behind social networks which include friends, families, and a broad lattice of familiar acquaintances. The transition to higher education is more than a change of place, however. For many it is associated with a transition to economic independence or a change in role or identity. While often written about in terms of challenge or difficulty, the transition to higher education, and higher education itself, equally offers what Oakeshott described as "the gift of an interval" (Oakeshott, 1989, p. 10). In this sense the university is more than an ordeal to encounter and survive, but, as Mahon puts it, "a time and place of refuge" where students can explore and share different roles, ideas, identities, and experiences "without fear of repercussions from the outside world" (Mahon, 2021, p. 2).

Transitions themselves are not inherently positive or negative. They can be challenging or enriching and often are both. Those transitions which are seen as positive, such as the transition to university, can equally be difficult and entail some cost. These costs include financial costs, but also the emotional costs associated with mismatched expectations or anticipatory stress. A mismatch in student expectations of what university will be like, and their initial experiences of higher education, has been shown to be associated greater levels of disengagement and attrition (Krause, 2005). Anticipatory stress, including concerns about study and exam pressures and financial concerns, is also associated with transition and change (ReachOut Australia, 2022). After decades of didactic teaching and direction in primary and secondary education, many students can struggle with the self-direction and independence of higher education (Winn, 2002).

What is clear is that the transition to higher education can require support. This is particularly true for students who struggle with their mental health. A study of all undergraduate students in Australia found that students with mental health difficulties were more vulnerable to dropout than their peers (Zając et al., 2024). The authors found that among students receiving treatment for their mental health, 22.2 per cent dropped out in their first year, compared to just 13.9 per cent of students not receiving mental health treatment (Zając et al., 2024). Another Australian study, this time conducted by the Australian Government's "Productivity Commission", identified mental health difficulties as particularly disruptive in the transition to higher education (Productivity Commission, 2020). This they attribute to "missed opportunities" (Productivity Commission, 2020, p. 161) at earlier stages of development, including poorer attendance and poorer academic outcomes at second level, which can leave students with mental health difficulties feeling further behind upon entering university.

Most recent statistics on non-progression indicate that 15 per cent of first year undergraduates do not progress to their second year (Higher Education Authority, 2024c). This figure from the 2021/2022 academic year represents a significant increase in student drop out, with this increase attributed to a number of factors including mental health difficulties linked to disengagement, long commutes, and reduced access to student support. Student counselling services report a surge in isolation, loneliness, and disconnection, particularly amongst first year students

(O'Brien, 2023), with long waiting lists building up in most university counselling services (O'Brien, 2024). Dropping out of college can result in a financial cost for students. Students who drop out in their first semester have to pay half the annual fees, while students who leave from January onwards have to pay the full fees (Higher Education Authority, 2024b). Further, students who start university, realise they are on the wrong course, and drop out, lose their eligibility for the "Free Fees" scheme and have to pay full tuition for the remainder of their undergraduate education (Higher Education Authority, 2024b). Struggling in the transition to higher education can come at cost – both personal and financial.

The transition to higher education is unique to each individual and to each generation. There is a tendency amongst university leavers to assume that the transition to higher education is similar to those experienced by previous generations. While many of the rituals of transition, from freshers' weeks to inductions to a packed social calendar, are the same as they were for previous intakes, each cohort faces a unique set of challenges and opportunities. This was most clearly seen during the COVID-19 pandemic when many students did not step onto campus until their second or third year. Other long-term trends, such as a precarious job market and greater availability of a skilled workforce, mean that many students will face short-term or contract-based employment upon graduation (Chesters et al., 2019). Ireland's housing crisis has meant that many can't afford to rent or stay near university and many Irish adults are now living at home into their 30s, which impacts not just life transitions but their sense of personal control and independence (Maguire, 2023). This has led many school leavers to report a lack of understanding from parents and schools about the pressures, realities, and difficulties they face (Fava and Baker, 2022). As more and more students transition to higher education with a mental health difficulty, it is important now more than ever to understand this experience.

The experience of transition

The accounts of the 27 students with mental health difficulties who shared their experiences reveal the vulnerability and opportunity of the transition to higher education. For some it was a transition filled with promise and optimism, while for others it was the moment when things "fell apart" (John). Millie, for example, describes the transition as "a stressful time" but says "it was a nice stress … I was looking forward to it". She feels that after "three years of having a really hard time" with her mental health as a teenager, she feels she is able to "enjoy" and "value" her time in higher education "because I didn't think I'd actually be here".

After an 18-year gap, during which he struggled with paranoid schizophrenia,[1] Leon returned to full-time education. Beginning with two years with the National Learning Network, a supported training centre, followed by a one-year university access course, Leon is now in the first year of his degree. He talked about how at each step along his higher education journey he has been supported and encouraged, and described "the attention and care and encouragement and facilities and infrastructure" he has received as he transitions to higher education as "wonderful". Leon says, "it was great to have that facility where I could go from being a stoner and a waster" to being a full-time student.

Joseph also took a more indirect route to higher education. After a gap of 20 years, he completed a one-year university access course at a local further education college but says that, although the access course prepared him well, he found university "much more stressful". He says he felt "very isolated and vulnerable" as a mature student in a class with "19 year old kids", and although he is now well into his second year Joseph says, "I still feel like that".

J. D. feels that making friends was "very important" in supporting his transition to higher education. He also says that loving his course "makes things easier". Fiona, too, says that making "an effort to meet people" during the first few weeks of college helped her make the transition: "I think I surprised myself with how well I coped with such a big change".

However, for some students, the transition to university was more challenging. Alicia describes how she "hit college" and "it all sort of triggered it [her anxiety and depression] again".

> The whole thing was a major shock to me.
>
> (Alicia)

Alicia says the large, crowded lectures "freaked me out" and caused her panic attacks to come "back again quite badly". It wasn't long before she "wasn't going to college". John says that "as soon as I started college my mental health fell apart".

> I was really depressed, really anxious, couldn't function here in college, I was overwhelmed. My shakes were back, I wasn't able to control my thoughts and the words would come into my head "I'm not intelligent", "I'm not

> meant to be here", "how did I get in here" […] suicide kept crossing my mind and it came to a point where I wasn't able to do my work.
>
> (John)

John says it was at this point that he decided to go back on medication and says that "within a few days of taking my tablets I felt better" and was able to get "back on track" in terms of his college work.

Ella described how she "dropped off the grid" when she moved away from home to attend college. She left the support system which had been in place since she was a teenager and, following the advice of her psychologist, "didn't register with the disability service": "the preventative measures that had been put in place for me at 16 … were just completely undone". She found herself away from home "with no help, trying to pretend it [her mental health difficulty] didn't exist". Ella struggled to meet people she "clicked with"; didn't enjoy the course she was on; found herself living in a stressful living environment with strangers; and, shortly after she started college, her relationship with her boyfriend "started to fall apart": "everything got terrible and I ended up just not going to college from January onwards". Ella dropped out of college at this point and returned the following September to start a course "which I enjoyed". She says the second transition "was still hard, but it was less hard, it kinda felt like I was on the path to becoming a bit better which was good".

Robert described how he struggled with the transition to college. He was "brilliant in school, like, top of my year" but when he got to college he realised "I actually had to work". This increase in difficulty coincided with an increase in freedom as Robert got his first part-time job which financed an active social life: "I was like Yahooo!": "Then I failed and I realised, oh you are top of the class in school but you are just standard in college". This failure "was crushing" for Robert and, failing again in second year, he decided to drop out.

Marie described how she "felt a bit lost" when she started college. She says she "banded together" with two girls from her secondary school with whom she had little in common and, during the first few weeks of college, "I was going out a lot, drinking a lot and it just wasn't me". It wasn't long before Marie found herself "worn out [and] exhausted" and decided to seek help from the student counselling service.

While the majority of students transitioned to university directly from secondary school, five of the 27 students made the transition as mature students. Others, like Ella and Robert, struggled the first time they transitioned to university and dropped out. They returned at a later stage and experienced the transition a second time with a greater degree of success. Many of those students who transitioned directly from secondary school did so through the Disability Access Route to Education (DARE) scheme.

Disability Access Route to Education (DARE)

Many of the students featured in this book entered university "through the DARE system" (Sophie). In Ireland, secondary school students sit the Leaving Certificate examinations in their final year. A minimum of six subjects are examined, with

English, Mathematics, and Irish being compulsory. Subjects can be taken at one of three levels and points are awarded based on the level of study and the grade awarded in the final exam. For example, the highest grade at higher level (H1) is awarded 100 points while the highest grade at ordinary level (O1) is awarded 56 points (Central Applications Office, 2024). The total number of points awarded across the student's six chosen subjects determines the number of points with which they can apply to higher education. The Central Applications Office (CAO) processes applications for entry to undergraduate courses in Irish Higher Education Institutions (HEIs) based on the student's number of points, with the more in-demand courses and universities requiring higher points for entry. The DARE scheme was introduced "as a third level alternative admissions scheme for school-leavers whose disabilities have had a negative impact on their second level education" (Access College, 2024). It offers reduced points places to school leavers who can (a) provide evidence of their disability and (b) demonstrate that their disability has had a negative impact on their secondary schooling (Access College, 2024). The opportunities and limitations of this approach to achieving equality of access to higher education are discussed in more detail in Chapter 2. Eight students spoke about their experience of coming through the DARE scheme, but it is likely that other participants availed of the scheme without it featuring in the stories they chose to share.

Sophie says she got into college "by the skin of my teeth". DARE represented a lucky break for her, although she does say she "was actually quite disappointed by the system". She explained her understanding of how the system works as follows:

> Basically you tick a box saying that you have a disability; you provide the paperwork … verifying from whoever it is, your doctor or psychiatrist, stating that you have a disability. Then all the people with disabilities, whether it's cancer or dyslexia, all go into a separate points race. […] About a fifth of places are reserved for mature, HEAR and DARE students. And basically they'll say we have two places here reserved for DARE students in this course, who has the highest points out of those with disabilities who applied?
>
> (Sophie)

Sophie felt disappointed because she believed that the DARE scheme meant that the entry points for a course would be reduced, granting equal access to all students with disabilities, but "it's not necessarily that they lower [the points], it's a separate points race". Sophie felt let down upon this realisation and wonders if she would have had a better shot at her first-choice course had she remained in the regular Central Applications Office (CAO) points race.

Millie, in contrast to Sophie, says the DARE scheme "gave me about sixty points, maybe seventy points, so I got 410 [points] and the course was 480 [points] I think, I'm not sure". For J. D. it mattered a lot that he "got in off my own bat": "The fact that, even though I got DARE and I would have been in anyway, that I got in by myself".

Lauren, however, says she "definitely wouldn't have got into college" on the points she earned in her Leaving Certificate examination and says that "no one expected me to get into college so that was great". For Claire, coming in through the DARE scheme leaves her feeling that she was "lucky" and with a sense that she "should overcompensate".

> I need to prove I can do well if I try, and it's not that I'm just lucky to be where I am and I kind of slipped in the door.
>
> (Claire)

This feeling of slipping in the door, as Claire puts it, is one described by many DARE students. By virtue of entering university through he DARE scheme, students are at increased risk of segregation or stigmatisation (Padden and Tonge, 2018). It can leave many students feeling isolated and excluded, as if imposters on a course with students who scored higher points in their Leaving Certificate. It has also been suggested that a process that focuses primarily on a student's difficulties and inability to perform on a par with their peers can lead to a lack of confidence amongst DARE students (Padden and Tonge, 2018).

Although Claire says she feels her getting a place in college was down to luck, she feels grateful "because if I didn't do DARE" she feels she would have ended up doing "a level 7 [further education course] or something, something I didn't want to do" which would have "really hit my confidence".

> It's terrible how the past years have been but I'm where I wanted to be. It worked out better than I thought it could.
>
> (Claire)

Conclusion

This chapter focused on the experience of transition. While the subject of a considerable body of research on higher education, it is interesting to note that there is no single definition of what a transition is. It can be understood as a period in time, encapsulating the early weeks of a student's first semester at university with all their "fresher" rituals and rites of passage. Transition can equally be understood as a process – one which each student goes through at their own pace and which recognises the varying degree of resources and preparedness available to each individual. Both conceptualisations of transition are represented in the students' accounts of their transition to university. Marie described how she "felt a bit lost" during those early weeks at university and how her efforts to adjust and fit in came at great personal cost. For Robert and Ella, transition was something they struggled with the first time and, in both instances, they dropped out before the end of their first year. For these students, transition was a process – one which took more than one attempt. Students who transitioned to university through the DARE scheme described how "lucky" (Claire) they were to get onto their courses in a way that recognised the adversity they had faced at second level. This route, however, left many feeling like they had gotten in "by the skin of my teeth" (Marie) and that they "should overcompensate" and "prove I can do well if I try, and it's not that I'm just lucky to be where I am and I kind of slipped in the door" (Claire). Students who transition to university through the DARE scheme are encouraged to register with their university disability service. This service, and students' experience of its supports, forms the focus of the next chapter.

4
Disability support

Learning objectives

1. **To analyse the opportunities and implications of diagnosis for students with mental health difficulties** and gain insights into the longer-term implications of having a psychiatric diagnosis.
2. **To identify the risks and challenges of disclosing a mental health difficulty for students studying professional courses**, such as social work or mental health nursing, that are underpinned by "fitness to practise" requirements.

Introduction

The inclusion of students with mental health difficulties in higher education in Ireland is currently based on a model of disability support. The opportunities and limitations of this model have been discussed in the previous chapters, as have efforts to move towards a more universal design for learning approach to inclusion. This chapter "parks" these important, albeit theoretical, debates and instead focuses on the experience of students whose engagement with higher education is facilitated, indeed "held together" (John), by disability support. It begins by exploring the experience of receiving a psychiatric diagnosis – an official prerequisite for access to supports and resources under the Fund for Students with Disabilities (FSD). It then examines student experiences of disability support itself – the aspects they availed of and "the practical stuff" (Mai) that supports them in achieving their academic goals. Finally, this chapter considers the experience of students who are studying a mental health-related course and the particular challenges they face in navigating the territory between lived experience and fitness to practise.

Diagnosis

All 27 students who shared their experiences of navigating higher education with a mental health difficulty as part of this book had received a formal diagnosis. Thirteen spoke at length about what it was like to receive a diagnosis, what it meant, and how it altered their experience. Students described how a diagnosis validated their distress. Ashley described how receiving her diagnosis of bipolar disorder "gave my difficulties, that I think were always belittled, some credit".

> At the beginning I was really happy because it validated that I wasn't making this up, like that this was actually a problem.
>
> (Adrianna)

Sophie spoke about she had "to fight very hard" for a diagnosis and for validation. She described how, upon initial assessment as a teenager, she "met some of the criteria" but not enough to receive a formal diagnosis of depression. She said she "found it very difficult throughout that time because I felt that everything that I had struggled with wasn't validated". She felt that her experience "justified some kind of medical reason as opposed to 'you just can't cope with your life'". Sophie described the "relief" when three years later, at 17, she was diagnosed with depression: "it was nice to have that feeling of validation and acknowledgement". Mary described how a diagnosis helped "other people take [her anxiety] a bit more seriously": "I feel it's a relief when I can say to someone, I'm feeling really anxious at the moment" (Mary).

A diagnosis also offered students a way of making sense of their experiences. Alicia described how "it was better than just thinking you are actually insane" while J. D. said that knowing what it was "named the monster": "it wasn't as scary anymore because it had a name". Ashley is grateful that "I now know what is going on" and that "there's a reason for it and it's not just my fault". This sense of "its not my fault" was also hugely beneficial for Claire:

> When I was diagnosed with depression, straight away a big weight felt lifted because it was just, it's not just how I feel, it's like, it's something wrong with me and I can be fixed.
>
> (Claire)

In addition to validating their experiences, offering some meaning, and a sense that "it's not just my fault" (Ashley), students acknowledged that a diagnosis was an essential step in accessing support: "I didn't care what he [psychiatrist] said to me, you know, I just wanted him to do something for me" (John).

Some students expressed concern about diagnosis. Sarah suggested that "once you have one diagnosis you end up with ten – every time you go in you get a different one". A diagnosis, for

Sarah, is quickly followed with a corresponding prescription; "every time you go to the doctor you get a different one and you're on different medications". Lauren also described receiving multiple diagnoses: "they throw them all at you". She disagrees with her current diagnosis of borderline personality disorder: "I'm like, you literally give that to everyone".

These concerns are further compounded by the fact that, over the longer term, psychiatric diagnoses are notoriously difficulty to shed. Even if a student has moved through a period of distress, their medical and other administrative records will continue to be marked with disorders that may limit their ability to, amongst other things, obtain a mortgage (McInerney, 2021), access life insurance (Mind, 2022), secure a visa to certain countries such as Australia or the US (Australian Government Department of Home Affairs, 2021), and/or pursue certain careers. These careers include professional careers such as medicine or the military where a diagnosis may undermine a person's application for selection or fitness to practise (Government of Ireland, 2007; Ministry of Defence, 2018). However, for those students who shared their experiences, the validation, meaning, and access to much-needed support provided by a diagnosis was at the forefront of their minds. These supports were accessed through their university disability support service.

Disability support service

Every university or higher education institute in Ireland has its own disability support service. These services are staffed by skilled disability support officers who are tasked, primarily, with administering the Fund for Students with Disabilities (FSD) but, professionally, with supporting students with disabilities to engage with and succeed in higher education. Anecdotally, disability support staff would say that as the demand for disability support increases (an increase of 273 per cent in 13 years (AHEAD, 2023)), ever greater proportions of their time are devoted to administration, at the expense of one-to-one time with students themselves. This is compounded by the fact that the FSD does not provide for the salaries of the disability support officers who administer the fund and these roles are, instead, the responsibility of universities to fund amidst a crisis of underfunding (Irish Universities Association, 2023). Despite these challenges, university disability support services provide an effective and, as described by many below, essential service to students with mental health difficulties.

Louise described how her consultant psychiatrist "advised" her to register with her college's disability service. She says, "I didn't know what to expect from the disability", and when, during her first meeting with the disability co-ordinator, he asked her "what supports are you looking for?" she didn't feel that she needed any.

> I wasn't there looking for supports, you know, it would be different if I had dyslexia or, I don't know, I was hard of hearing or that type of thing ... like, I didn't need anything.
>
> (Louise)

John, in contrast, says that without the various supports available to him through his college disability service "my life would fall apart within 24 hours". He attends the college GP "on a regular basis" and receives one-to-one academic writing support which "makes a huge difference". John puts his successes in college "down to the people around me" as well as his own effort and determination: "I'm merely an individual that can't function without the help of other people".

Mai also says, "I think I'm doing so well because the disability service is there". Through her university's disability support service Mai is able to access the support of an occupational therapist who helps her with "the practical stuff" around drawing up study timetables and breaking down assignments into manageable chunks. Students who were able to access the services of an occupational therapist service spoke very highly of the support it offered. Joseph, Greg, Mai, Fiona, and Millie each spoke about how "helpful" occupational therapy was.

> [The occupational therapist] helped organise my time and task management which in turn took the stress away from me because when I had everything organised […] It took a weight off my shoulders.
>
> (Joseph)

Other supports mentioned by the students as being beneficial included access to a separate, smaller, exam centre; access to quiet spaces on campus where the students can take time out; "library privileges" (Sophie); and an additional "printing allowance" (Millie). A separate exam centre seemed particularly important for the students: "you don't have to go to the RDS [exam centre] where there's like 3000 people. It's a small room with 20 people … it makes a huge difference you know" (Joseph).

Students who entered university through the DARE scheme were encouraged to register with their university disability service as soon as they accepted their college place. Others were referred to the service by their tutors or other academic staff members; the student counselling service; their university psychiatrist; and/or their own psychiatrist/mental health team. Some students were encouraged to register with the disability support service upon returning to college after a period "off books" [officially off the college register for a period of time] due to mental health difficulties.

Perhaps the greatest value of being registered with their college disability service, one that emerged repeatedly in the students' narratives, was the sense of reassurance or "comfort" (Millie) that being registered offered them; a sense of knowing there is a port should they ever encounter a storm.

> Just knowing that … if you really do need it, there is support there.
>
> (Millie)

Studying a mental health related subject as a student with a mental health difficulty

Many students with experience of distress are, perhaps understandably, interested in the subjects of mental health, psychology, social work/social studies, or mental health nursing. This is often motivated by a desire "to say I understand it" (Adrianna) and/or a desire to "use what I've learned to help other young people" (Niamh). The experiences described below are set against a backdrop where the rights of a person to study or work in an area of their choosing are offset against professional "fitness to practise" standards set by professional registration bodies in psychology, social work, and mental health nursing (Campbell et al., 2022; Goldberg, Hadas-Lidor, and Karnieli-Miller, 2015; Manthorpe and Stanley, 1999; Stanley et al., 2011). For those students who disclose their mental health difficulty, and access support for a university disability support service, the support they receive is tinged with the risk that it might comprise their fitness to practise or "professional veneer", as Mary puts it. This section explores, firstly, students' interest in studying a mental health-related course and their desire to help other in similar situations to theirs. It then visits the experiences of those students who are negotiating the transition from service user to service provider – sometimes, as is the case for Louise, in the same mental health service. Finally, it considers the wider implications for students of being identified as having a mental health difficulty at this formative juncture in their professional lives.

Ten of the 27 students who participated in this research were studying a mental health-related course. Six were studying psychology – three at undergraduate level (Adrianna, Thomas, Sophie) and three at postgraduate level (Kate, Mary, Niamh). The remaining four were studying mental health nursing (Faye, Louise, Mai) and social work (Annie).

Adrianna spoke about how, for her, studying psychology is a means of getting the "qualification" to back up the knowledge and understanding she has gained through experience: "being able to say 'I understand it'". She was drawn to the area because she feels that a therapeutic "relationship was one of the most important things in my life … and [I want to] give back a little of what I've been given". She says that this "sounds soppy" but, unlike her fellow psychology students, Adrianna hopes to enter the profession with the understanding that she "can't really help people" rather "be there with people and help them get through what they're going through and just be that person, maybe the first person people talk to".

Annie described how her school guidance counsellor told her, "Oh God, you can't be a social worker – you're mentally unwell". Many of the students spoke about how they were discouraged from studying a mental health-related course on the grounds of having experienced distress themselves. Annie says she doesn't "think it's fair to say that because I have had things in my life" that she shouldn't go on to fulfil her childhood ambition to become a social worker. She feels she has "more experience to deal with other people's hardships when I've been through my own". Annie believes that having "somebody who can actually relate to the client" would be a really useful addition to any mental health team.

> I don't think it's fair to ask every social worker to be in tip-top condition when they are dealing with people who aren't.
>
> (Annie)

One of the most defining features of the students who participated in this research more generally was their desire to help others. For some, such as Adrianna (above) and Leon, this was motivated by a desire give back. Leon described the "attention and care and encouragement and facilities and infrastructure and income" he has been afforded in his life as "wonderful", particularly, he says, "for someone who hadn't done much for anybody". For Leon, the charity he and his partner set up to raise funds for a local children's hospital is his opportunity to give back to a "society [that] has been very good to me". Ashley spoke about how a traumatic experience in her teens left her with a sense that "Oh my God, I'm a horrible person, I deserve nothing": "I decided at that point I was going to try and get medicine and be a doctor because that's the only way I could make it up to the world". She felt that by working hard to "try and help people" that "that might make up for the bad thing that I'm after doing". Although she didn't "get medicine", Ashley spoke about how she hopes to use her current degree to find a way "to give back to the mental health community" that she feels has helped her so much.

Niamh described how studying psychology offered her an opportunity to combine her "own experience" with intellectual learning in order to "apply what I know, what I've experienced with research" so that she may help other young people who may struggle with their mental health.

> I just want to use what I've learned to help other young people and show them that recovery is possible.
>
> (Niamh)

Mary described how helping others, particularly through her postgraduate psychology research, creates a sense of "meaning" that is very important in her life.

> Helping people in some small way, like if you can even help one person, if you could change one person's life, then it will have been worth it.
>
> (Mary)

The meaning offered by helping others was particularly important to Thomas. He says, "I just want to help people, it's all I want to do", and adds, "I would not see any purpose in life if I could not help people". Over the course of his two conversational interviews, Thomas mentioned 13 groups, charities, voluntary organisations, and extra-curricular activities that he has been involved in over the last two years and says that giving back to his community and helping others makes him "feel like my life [has] meaning to it".

For those students studying mental health nursing, having personal experience created a number of additional difficulties. The exception to this was Faye who appears not to have disclosed or discussed the mental health problems she experienced as a teenager with any of her course co-ordinators. She feel that this experience doesn't impact on her mental health nurse training except to give her unique "insight" into issues such as self harm and personality disorders. Louise and Mai's experiences, however, appear to have been less smooth.

Louise says she "always had it in my head to do nursing" and after she finished school she did a pre-nursing course and later worked as a care assistant before applying for a mature-entry place to study nursing at university: "I applied for general, intellectual disability and psych[iatric], the three types". While she was unsuccessful the first time, after two years as a care assistant she was offered a place on a mental health nursing degree course at the university that was linked with the mental health services she was still regularly attending.

> I found out then that it was psych I got and it was great news, I was really, really happy but really, really afraid as well.
>
> (Louise)

She immediately went to see her consultant who offered to "suss out" the most appropriate course of action with contacts at the university: "he was advised to tell me to make sure I'm honest in application forms, honesty really was what they were saying was the big thing. Register early with the disability service ... that was basically it". When filling in the paper work, Louise was careful to be honest but brief; "If they wanted to know more well they could ask but I wasn't giving away anything really that could stop my chances".

While her consultant was happy to provide written verification of Louise's fitness to undertake a nursing degree course, she received what she experienced as opposition from other facets within the college. These included the disability officer she had been assigned ("He was already insinuating that because of the background I have I'm going to act crazy"); occupational health ("She said to me 'As you are sitting here in front of me now are you thinking of killing yourself?'"); and her clinical placement co-ordinator ("the CPC said 'Louise [Surname], you are not the girl who had all the trouble with occupational health are you?'"). In spite of this opposition Louise has successfully completed her placements and exams. While she enjoys her time on placement, she sometimes does "find it, kind of, pulls on me in ways. There is people there who just draw me straight back to everything". Louise has successfully negotiated the first half of her first year but says she is "constantly" on edge – aware that "this can be taken away on me" should she slip up in the slightest.

Like Louise, Mai studied a pre-nursing course and, when completing her college admissions form the following year, "put down general nursing first and then psychiatric nursing". She says that now she's "delighted I got my psychiatric nursing instead of general". Mai feels her own experience allows her to "empathise really well with the patients": "I understand what it's like, how scary it is to have a panic attack because you do think you are going to die". She says that "when I am on placement I'm happy" and knows that mental health nursing is something "I will like working in". However, she also says that "placement can be hard" – particularly when she sees patients with "similar" problems "getting help" and "getting better": "you are like, Oh my God, why can't mine get better". Mai was discouraged from disclosing her mental health problem while on placement and gets "annoyed" with the sense of hypocrisy that lingers in the mental health field.

> You are either a nurse or a patient, like you can't have mental illness while you're a nurse. [You're told you] should practice what you preach and yet it's still like that's "them", the mentally ill, and we're "us" and we're, like, immune to it.
>
> (Mai)

Mary also appears to be painfully aware of the stigma around being a mental health professional with a mental health difficulty. She spoke about how she wouldn't seek help for her depression and anxiety in the college where she was doing her postgraduate research because she feels that "whether you realise it or not sometimes people can use it against you".

Mary: You're trying to maintain that professional, I don't know, veneer. No one is going to take you seriously if they think you deal with a mental health problem. And that is the reality of it. I'm not ashamed of it but it's how other people perceive you, you can't control how they're going to see it. […] It would be difficult to be taken seriously. They'd be like "oh, that person has a mental health problem", you know.

Emma: So you think that they would view you in a negative light?

Mary: Yeah. I think they would see you as less professional, less competent.

What this section reveals is that studying a mental health-related subject with current or previous experience of a mental health difficulty is not straightforward. The empathy and desire to help described by the students position them to be excellent caregivers, but the toll of supporting those with experiences similar to theirs is considerable for some. This is further compounded by the fear that "this can be taken away from me" (Louise) should their diagnosis or distress be revealed, and concern that their professionalism may be undermined by the regrettable stigma associated with mental health difficulties.

Conclusion

This chapter explored just how students with mental health difficulties are supported in Irish universities. It described students' experience of receiving a diagnosis and the supports they availed themselves of through their university disability support service. This chapter also touched on the challenges associated with receiving a psychiatric diagnosis and, in particular, the implications of being registered as disabled for students undertaking professional courses related to mental health. Overall, what this chapter highlights is that while the benefits of being able to avail of additional supports such as occupational therapy or extra time in exams is undeniably valuable, indeed essential, for the students in this study, they are not without consequence.

5
The lived experience of navigating higher education with a mental health difficulty

Learning objectives

1. **To understand the lived experience of students with mental health difficulties** and the meaning that these students ascribe to their higher education experience.
2. **To identify the day-to-day challenges experienced by university students with mental health difficulties** and gain insights into the practical measures students adapt to deal with these challenges.
3. **To evaluate the impact of perfectionism on the well-being and university experience of students with mental health difficulties** and examine the function of perfectionism for these students.

Introduction

Thus far, this book has focused primarily on the experiences of students with mental health difficulties in terms of the policies, pathways, and provisions designated to support their inclusion and success in higher education. This chapter focuses instead on the experience of students themselves. It examines the nature and meaning of higher education for the students who participated in this study, as well as the day-to-day reality of managing a mental health difficulty. It reflects students' attempts to come to terms with their distress, "accepting that this is your life", as Adrianna put it, and "learning how to manage it" (Ella), all while navigating higher education. While undoubtedly challenging, and mired with the reality that "I don't think it will ever be fixed" (Ashley), many students in this book spoke about the upside of "it" – their particular mental health difficulty or distress.

The nature and meaning of higher education for students with mental health difficulties

This book sought to understand the nature and meaning of higher education for Irish students with mental health difficulties. This ambition reflects its hermeneutic phenomenological orientation and commitment to getting as close as possible to the experience as it is lived. The method by which this is achieved is represented in Appendix, and the broader body of work from which these accounts stem can be seen in its entirety elsewhere (Farrell, 2022b; Farrell and Mahon, 2021). This section presents student descriptions of their experience at university and the meaning they ascribe to higher education in their lives. It provides day-to-day examples of the unique challenges students face in a university setting as well as what higher education, and education in general, means to them.

Beginning with the students' lived experience of navigating higher education; the students' accounts were peppered with struggles directly related to their mental health problems. These included the challenge to concentrate and stay focused (Claire, Greg, James); the struggle to attend lectures (Lauren, Claire); the effort required to stir up motivation or interest in their work when their mood was low (Greg, James); and the battle with perfectionism, procrastination, and getting work in on time (Adrianna, Ella, Greg, Robert, Mai, Louise, Joseph, Ashley, James, Claire).

Lauren described the thin line she walks between "not eating" and not failing her continuous assessment assignments and examinations. She described how she "failed [first] year on attendance" even before she reached the end of the first term and took the advice of her tutor who "suggested going off-books and doing medical repeat". She "got through" first year the second time round and, now, in her second year, says that her anorexia nervosa is presenting "a bit of a problem, but not to the extent – I don't think I'll fail. I hope not, because I'm definitely not repeating […] I think I'll just about make it, I think".

While for Lauren every day involves a balancing act between the demands of her eating disorder and the demands of her degree, Sophie faces a similar balancing act but in her case it is between her introversion and social anxiety and getting a degree. Sophie says, "I need to get an education, you know?" but describes the "academic setting" and "class situation" as "very daunting": "Having to socialise and chat to people and stuff, I was very intimidated". After dropping out of college at her first attempt, Sophie came "back into a situation that I knew I wouldn't be comfortable in 100 per cent[,] knowing that there wasn't really a way out for me". She described how she is "learning all the time how to cope better" with her anxiety but feels she has "no choice" but to do this if she is to get her degree: "I can't just not do anything for the rest of my life".

Sophie was one of eight students who described having to drop out or go "off-books" and either repeat a year or come back and start another course the following year. Ella struggled with the transition to college. Moving away from home she lost all her supports and was discouraged from registering with her university support services by her psychologist who felt "admitting to mental illness in the academic field would put a black mark on my name". She found herself living with strangers, one of whom she thinks "might have had some social issues", and doing "the wrong course". Ella also broke up with her boyfriend during this period and says that "everything got terrible and I ended up just not going to college … I got very depressed, very anxious. I got very, very anxious". Ella dropped out of college before the end of her first year: "it was the first time I'd ever really failed at anything in my life". Although Ella came back the next year and registered with her university support services, started a course that she enjoys, and found better living arrangements, she says, "I have a lot of insecurities about my academic work now" which she links to "how I dropped out of first year … I'd never failed anything before".

Greg, a second year PhD student, wonders if "the tendency towards the depression and anxiety is incompatible with academia".

> The academic environment is a high pressure environment and one in which you feel as if you are being criticised constantly and you are expected to, kind of, criticise yourself or motivate yourself.
>
> (Greg)

Greg finds that this pressure, combined with a lack of structure, "takes its toll". He is currently struggling with depression and becoming increasingly "disillusioned" with academic life. So much so, that at the time of interview, Greg had decided to drop out of his PhD programme.

James, also studying for a PhD, described similar struggles to Greg – particularly when he first started his research. He spoke about feeling "quite depressed, very low motivation, wasn't working hard at what I was doing, wasn't interested". James says that one thing that helped him come out of his low phase was the realisation that, "if I fail the whole PhD and everything goes out the window, I didn't have one [a PhD] starting so that's OK". He says he "can't afford to obsess over my PhD" as he "can't bounce back the way other people can" and feels that maintaining perspective and "awareness" is important for him and his mental health.

Adrianna says she came into college with "a lot of leftover stuff, like you know, throwing up and self-harm and depression and changes in medication". Now in her third year Adrianna feels that, although "I still have moments where things aren't great", ultimately she is "pushing forward": "It [the distress] comes back but it's not plaguing me every day". Adrianna described how she "loves the subject" she is studying and during her time in college has "used the resources" available to her and year by year feels she is becoming "more solid, more able to deal with things". Higher education appears to have offered Adrianna a supportive environment in which to grow and develop personally as well as academically. Higher education for Adrianna, and for many of the other students, represents much more than a qualification or a career boost.

The meanings students ascribe to their higher education experience are both highly personal and enormously significant. For John, education is the key to breaking the cycle of poverty and abuse he was born into. He says, "I really do see society or life as a kind of circle and it's very hard to get out of and I'm trying to get out of that circle". John described how he grew up "at the bottom of the pile" in terms of social class, with both parents unemployed and living on social welfare benefits.

> I don't want their [his parents'] lives, you know. I don't know what my life is going to turn out like or what way my life is going to go but at least I'm trying to give life a go.
>
> (John)

John described his early life as being dominated by "deprivation", "chaos", "coldness", "dampness", "poverty", "neglect", "emotional abuse", "verbal abuse" and "sexual abuse". By the time he reached his early 20s John was living alone, away from home, unemployed, "constantly living in really bad accommodation … I had no friends really, isolation and no qualifications or no education". One friend he did meet along the way was a man who "really emphasised the importance of education".

> He said to me "If you get your education nobody can take it away from you" and that's why I want to get it, I want to get something that nobody can take away from me.
>
> (John)

John's friend suggested he wasn't "able for college" right away but that he should begin with a level 4[1] qualification and "build it up" from there. John successfully completed his level 4 certificate, was offered a place on a one-year university access programme which, in turn, led him onto his honours degree course at that university. He is now in the second year of his degree and says, "I really like this new life".

> I'm trying to break that circle you know, I'm desperately trying to break it.
>
> (John)

Joseph told the story of how he "returned to college to fulfil a lifelong ambition" after almost 20 years out of the classroom. This move took a lot of courage for Joseph, particularly as he had struggled for all of his adult life with crippling anxiety and panic attacks. He described the first day of his one-year pre-college course "thinking oh God can I do it?".

> I was sitting there trembling and I remember pins and needles all over my hands and coming up my face and

> I, so many times nearly left the room. I was scared, nervous, twenty years since I was in a classroom.
>
> (Joseph)

But Joseph "hung in there" and after the pre-college course started on a four-year degree programme in university. University presented a number of significant challenges for Joseph and he says he gets "totally overwhelmed" at times, but he has a "passion" for his subject and hopes to continue to go a specialist master's degree in order to fulfil his "dream … to work in a museum".

Kate described how, even as a young girl, she thought deeply about the world and "questioned the meaning of life and why people are here and why people do what they do". Developing anorexia nervosa as a teenager curtailed her education, and although she "left school in 5th year" she sat her Leaving Certificate examination: "I failed the Leaving Cert but I did sit it". At a particularly low point in her early 20s, Kate says she "was very sick and I had tried to kill myself a number of times". During that time Kate "questioned a lot like the meaning of life and why people are here and why people do what they do" and, on the recommendation of a family friend, decided to travel to Pakistan to speak to a man "that many people go to for help". One of the things this sage-like man suggested to Kate was that she should pursue her passion for learning and knowledge.

> So when I was in Pakistan, this guy said to me, "Study", he said "study as much as you can, study and learn as much as you can" and in my head I was like "Yeah that's not possible".
>
> (Kate)

However, Kate "came back and started Googling possibilities and options of what I could study" and within weeks of returning from Pakistan started a degree with the Open University. Kate completed her degree and is currently in the first year of a two-year master's degree programme. Although she says she feels she is "winging it" and feels "like a fraud", education and learning for Kate have a much deeper significance: "sometimes I feel in my life I am to learn things intensely". In returning to education she "wanted to understand, I wanted to understand people, I wanted to understand myself".

> What I am doing is trying to form a path of some type of understanding or knowledge, like there is no way I am going to know everything or even much at all, but I am going to see what I can learn. If over the years I have been so willing to let go of this life in an instant, well then I need to understand why I should be here.
>
> (Kate)

While for Kate higher education offered her a chance to satisfy the deep curiosities and questions that had shaped her life, for Leon it offered him an opportunity to gain "social approval". He describes himself as "the black sheep", particularly after he was diagnosed with paranoid schizophrenia at the age of 18. He says, "it has been a long road but I'm getting there" and, after two years at the National Learning Network and one year doing a university access course, Leon is finally in the first year of his undergraduate degree. This offers him "the social acceptance of being a student" at a prestigious university which has "helped my mental health as well, you know, because I have that social approval now".

> I was the type of guy that your mother didn't want you hanging around with but now I'm the type of guy that everybody's mother would love to see [it's] as simple as that.
>
> (Leon)

This section has examined the challenges faced by students with distress in higher education. Some of these, such as the struggle to attend or to complete assignments on time, were more universal than others. However, each student's experience is unique and those represented above offer a glimpse into what it is like for certain students as they navigate their way through higher education.

The meaning of higher education extends far beyond the day-to-day challenges for many students. Indeed, it is this meaning that motivates many students to continue in the face of significant adversity. For John, education was his way out of the cycle of poverty and abuse he was born into. For Joseph, it was the chance to "fulfil a lifelong ambition" (p. 15). For Kate, education was a means of answering some of the bigger questions that shaped her life, particularly the question of whether life was truly worth living at all, while, for Leon, being a third level student offered him a chance to earn the social approval that he felt he lacked as a result of having a mental illness. While this section focused on the "what" (nature) and "why" (meaning) of student experience, the next examines the "how".

Managing a mental health difficulty while at university

One of the more defining features of students' accounts was the manner in which they managed and accommodated "it", their mental health difficulty, while at university. It appears the initial, and often most painful, first step in learning to live with and manage "it" was accepting "that this is in your hands" (Adrianna). Adrianna spoke about reaching the realisation that professionals "can only help you when you're in their office and that *you* have to get your shit together" [student emphasis].

> It's about accepting, I think first of all accepting that this is your life … [and secondly] figuring out that it's actually just you who can fix it.
>
> (Adrianna)

When Sophie first started "going through severe bouts of depression" as a teenager, she says, "I pitied myself and felt very much like 'poor me' – how will I ever cope with this?". She feels that this was "a perfectly natural response" to the injustice of her situation, "but at the same time I hated myself for not being resilient and for not somehow having the means to cope with it". Sophie described how she initially believed "everything will work out happily ever after" but "as the months went on" it became clear that this time the ending was unlikely to be quite as happy and straightforward as she hoped.

> I remember sitting there thinking there's no one coming on a while horse to save me. It really was a slap in the

> face. It was the first time I realised that I could be in serious trouble, because there was no help in sight [and] I didn't know how to help myself.
>
> (Sophie)

Sophie says that "for me as a young person it was the first time I was not equipped to handle what came my way and that was a very frightening feeling". She didn't realise that coping was "something that you learn".

Ella, Joseph, Lauren, Marie, Ashley, Claire, and James all spoke, unprompted, about how, once they had come to terms with the reality that "it's always going to be there" (Lauren), they can then "learn to manage it better" (Lauren).

Marie says, "I'm always going to have to look after myself and I find that frustrating sometimes but I think I just need to learn to deal with it".

> It's hard being a 23-year-old college student when you know you need to be in bed by 11 so you're not down the next day. You know? I need to watch what I eat, I need to make sure I exercise.
>
> (Marie)

Marie knows "the statistics aren't great" and feels that mental health problems are "always going to be part of my story", but she says that "every time it happens I learn a little bit more" and feels that right now she just needs to "keep working on figuring myself out – that's the plan".

Like Marie, Ashley says, "I don't think it'll ever be fixed" but feels that she needs to "make the adaptations and learn the strategies and things that are going to make things doable" in spite of her bipolar disorder. However, for Ashley, her "main problem is that being consistent gets boring". She says, "I do miss the element of chaos in my life" and since "things have gotten together" and have "been good recently" she feels she has "lost a chunk of identity". James also thinks "bipolar's for life" but he doesn't "think that means it has to control" him. These words reverberated in the story of Joseph, who says, "I don't think you can cure anxiety". He says that when "Bressie, the guy from the *Voice of Ireland* [TV show], stated that he suffered from anxiety and panic attacks, and it's gone, I actually felt jealous". Joseph described all the ways in which he has been "just trying to deal with it as well as I possibly could" since he was a teenager. It has been a long struggle for Joseph, but he says that "every step I took made a difference" and now, after "24 years of suffering", he is "managing my anxiety as well as it [can] be managed".

Ella described herself as "a ticking time bomb – there's always a chance I'll go bad again":

> I think to deny that it's going to be there forever is to turn your back on a tiger. It's not about recovery, it's about managing. It's about accepting it and also learning how to manage it and learning how to deal with it and to predict – in a way to predict the unpredictable".
>
> (Ella)

One thing that has been hard for both Ella and Mai to come to terms with is the sense of wonder they both have as to what might have been had they not had distress to contend with.

Ella says, "I should really get a first[-class]" honours degree but because of her daily struggles with anxiety and depression she says, "I'd be very surprised if I do": "what will annoy me will be it won't be a lack of capability, it will be having been so distracted and the mental, I do think the mental illness will have impacted it a lot". Mai spoke about how she had the opportunity to sit a scholarship exam which, had she been successful, would have meant that she "would have been able to move out of my house, not get verbally abused by my family" any more: "I couldn't do it in the end, I got too sick".

Students described a variety of way in which they manage their mental health on a day-to-day basis. These included developing routines and schedules to support their efforts to stay well. Marie identified early on that "structure is really good for me", and when her mental health really began to deteriorate she "had to get very good at making plans and schedules". James and Ashley both spoke at length about how "when I lose my structure I start to get stressed". For Ashley, "stress and alcohol are the two big things" that affect her moods and are the two things she is most learning to keep under control. James spoke about how he finds it "very difficult to establish a routine".

> When you miss sleep, and that was the worst one as well, where you could go for days with like four hours sleep a night, you were in way worse moods and then you're fuelling yourself with sugars throughout the day which is ups and downs all day long.
>
> (James)

For James, "bipolar's for life" but he can "manage it" ("I'll just continue with the diet, continue with the lifestyle and continue meditating") in the knowledge that "if you're not managing it, it could go out of control". Keeping busy is another important strategy for James, one which Sarah, Lauren, and Marie spoke about too: "it's probably better to be busy than to be not doing anything at all". For Lauren, living with "it" meant living within the limits of her eating disorder. She is very aware of "what I can and can't do" – something that her friends have become aware of too. She knows that, when her friends invite her for lunch, "I can go to Marks and Spencer's and there're two things I can have there; there's one thing I can have in Costa' that fits the calories I'm willing to have" (Lauren).

Sarah spoke about all the things she does to nurture her mental health: "I love art and I really find when I'm doing that it really helps, but it's hard to get the motivation to do that"; "I think using your hands really helps, like drawing and painting and I was doing a dressmaking class as well"; "I started basketball last week so hopefully that will help"; "I do keep myself very busy and my father and myself did the couch to 5 km and we go for runs together and I think that is really good"; "I do mindfulness every night, well, me and my mum do it as a 'workout'".

> I suppose what is frustrating me about everything is I try so hard to fight and beat it. Like, they tell you if you eat healthily, they tell you if you exercise and they tell you if you talk you're going to…but I do everything and get no relief.
>
> (Sarah)

Perfectionism

One of the great opportunities afforded by adopting a hermeneutic phenomenological approach was the opportunity to sit with, and listen to, the students as they themselves brought forth aspects of their experience important to them. In doing so they were able to draw "something forgotten into visibility" (Harman, 2007, p. 92). They gave voice to currents of influence often lost beneath the surface of "what happened". One example of this was the undercurrent of perfectionism in the experiences of 17 of the 27 students in particular.

The motivation for perfection, as described by the students, appeared to come from four, often inter-related, sources: an internal desire/drive for perfection; a desire to meet the perceived/actual expectations of others; a desire to prove themselves or to prove others wrong, and the fear their work, and/or they, were not "good enough". Each of these four driving factors will be discussed in turn.

A number of the students described how they would have, as Ashley put it, "very high standards" for themselves. Annie described how "growing up I was always the type who wanted good grades and things like that". She remembers winning her first Irish dancing trophy at the age of six and how she realised "I could actually do this and from then on it became something I wanted to do well in". Annie says that her parents never pushed her to do well at dancing or school; "It was very much myself, I was very competitive … it was a personal thing for myself, I wanted to do well".

Fiona also described how her parents "are always like 'all you can do is your best' but for me I am like 'no, I need to do better'". She says she is "very hard on myself, like, I push myself really hard".

Ashley's father "could never understand" why she pushed herself so hard to achieve in dancing and in school: "he just didn't think it was normal for a child to put themselves under the pressure I did". Like Annie, Ashley discovered that by working hard she did well in dancing competitions. Before third year in secondary school Ashley says school "wasn't a big deal" but when she achieved very high marks in her Junior Certificate "I realised I was kind of good at school so then that worry transferred from the dancing to my school [work]".

James spoke about his "all or nothing" attitude to life: "everything has to be the last thing in the world. You have to win every tackle, you have to win everything, you're a complete perfectionist". However, he identified that while this attitude has brought him considerable success in life, it also means "there's no kind of satisfaction at times".

> [I] just genuinely thought [that] anyone who's not striving for perfection is wasting this, that or the other and then realising they're much happier than you later on in life you kind of start figuring out this is a terrible way to lead your mind or lead your life.
>
> (James)

All four students identified how their internal drive to succeed was a double-edged sword. On the one hand they are all hugely successful young people but on the other hand the pressure they place themselves under could become "so overwhelming" (Fiona) at times. Annie described how in her Leaving Certificate year she was training for the world championships in dancing, working a part-time job "to fund my dance classes" and, at the same time, working hard in school to achieve the points she needed to get into university. Eventually it all became too much: "I couldn't really handle it I suppose".

Fiona has also struggled to keep up with the standards she sets herself. She described how at the end of the term prior to our interview she had to submit a number of big assignments on the same day. She "wanted to do really well in everything" and in the process "just worked way too hard … I did just burn out".

> It was just way too much for me and I was exhausted because I was working way too hard. And then I couldn't do anything because I was so tired.
>
> (Fiona)

Ashley also identified how the pressure she puts herself under can be "quite extreme".

> I like it to be, I don't know, just very, very high standards of perfectionism in all my college work to the point where it's kind of maybe frightening.
>
> (Ashley)

In school she placed herself under such pressure to achieve that when she went into her first Leaving Certificate exam she "had the most extreme panic attack". She says that the exams went "essentially downhill from there on" and, in the end, Ashley had to repeat the year in school and sit the Leaving Certificate a second time.

While Annie, Fiona, Ashley, and James described having high standards and expectations of themselves, a number of students spoke about feeling some degree of expectation from others. Adrianna said, "there was an expectation, it was probably never really kind of said and shouted at me, but there was an expectation that I'd always do really good at school". She feels that this expectation has "become so engrained that you don't even consider that you're doing it for someone [else]".

> You kind of think this is what you have to do, this is what you are, this is your goal. It's not even because I'm not going to go and show my mom that I got an A, I'm kind of like, OK, I have to get an A because if I don't get an A it's not good. I don't know, it's a bit messed up in that way.
>
> (Adrianna)

Like Adrianna, Lauren says, "I have this really bad perfectionism complex and it's such an issue, it's a ridiculous issue". She said that high expectations were "in our house" as she was growing up and she is "sure we're all a little bit like that [perfectionistic]".

> I remember one year I got a D in maths and I got As and Bs in everything else and I was like "Oh, they're [her parents] going to kill me, they're going to kill me".
>
> (Lauren)

From a very young age Lauren had set her sights on becoming a paediatrician. She says that, even now, she "would still be really interested" in going back to do medicine but during her Leaving Certificate year Lauren became aware that she "wasn't doing well" in some key subjects and was going to struggle to meet the entry requirements for medicine. Ultimately, she decided to "change the plan".

> I was worried that people would be disappointed because obviously it is a – you know like medicine's up here [gestures] … I mean our family; there'd be a lot of really intelligent people. So I don't know, like it would have been nice to be "up there" but its fine.
>
> (Lauren)

Thomas, too, felt the pressure of expectation as he entered his final year of secondary school.

> It was just this expectation … I felt like I was going to let everyone down because when you got to 6th year it was just constant … Like from the first week it was like "okay heads down". And that just, it killed me.
>
> (Thomas)

He described feeling a weight of expectation associated with being a high-achieving student in a school where few students go on to third level.

> All through secondary school there this constant look of … and from the teachers as well, and from everyone, it was just this perspective "Oh [Thomas] is going to do great in life" "[Thomas] is gonna go on to do this… [Thomas] is gonna go on to do that …".
>
> (Thomas)

By the second week of his final year, Thomas was leaving classes "in tears". He wasn't sleeping, had lost his appetite, and stopped going out and getting involved in his normal activities. Within two months of starting sixth year he had been diagnosed with "severe depression" and prescribed a series of psychiatric medications.

Three students described how their drive to achieve perfection comes as a result of a deep desire to prove others wrong. In Sarah's case, the person she wanted to prove wrong was her secondary school guidance counsellor. The guidance counsellor suggested Sarah be placed in a lower class as she felt that her dyslexia would prevent Sarah from keeping up in school.

> I think I spent all of my school years trying to prove that woman wrong and I did prove her wrong and I'm still proving her wrong, you know.
>
> (Sarah)

Sarah says, "I think there must be a link there [between] that whole thing of proving people wrong and being a perfectionist".

> I am always trying to prove others and myself wrong, you know.
>
> (Sarah)

For Niamh it was her grandmother, who made it clear that she had low expectations of Niamh from a young age, that she wanted to prove wrong.

> [She would say] "Oh, you're never going to be good enough, you're not going to make anything of your life,

> you're going to stay the way you are" ... I just wanted to prove her wrong.
>
> (Niamh)

Claire described how she "wanted to prove that I could do it". When she was in school Claire struggled with depression and anxiety to the point that, in her final year, she attended a total of just 33 days "and the days I was in, I left early". In spite of this Claire says, "I wanted to do well in my Leaving Cert and I wanted to prove myself and I wanted to do the best that I could". She says that even today she still tries to "overcompensate" and constantly worries that she is "a bit behind people".

> I need to prove that I can do well if I try and it's not that I'm just lucky to be where I am.
>
> (Claire)

The fourth, and perhaps the strongest, force that appeared to motivate students' drive for perfection was fear – fear that their work, and/or they, were not good enough.

Greg described how he doesn't "feel particularly anxious as long as I can, I suppose, compare to other people nearby and convince myself that I am doing better than them". He spoke about how as an undergraduate he "wanted to be liked" by his lecturers; "I really wanted to be seen to be understanding and doing well". However, while this desire to be liked and to do well placed him at the top of his class it also led to him experiencing deep anxiety, particularly when it came to submitting assignments:

> I was crippled by anxiety that they would, you know, think that I was a kind of a bit of a, that I was a failure or

they were disappointed that I could have done better in it.

(Greg)

Greg described immobilising procrastination: "I suppose I have had difficulty with just getting rid of [assignments] at the deadline and instead going 'oh no, it's not ready it's not done'". By the time he reached his final year Greg struggled to submit anything on time for fear that the "assignments were going to fail". Assignments and extensions continued to pile up for Greg until eventually he "withdrew from college to repeat".

Adrianna, too, described how she "wanted to do really well and wanting it [her work] to be perfect because I wanted to show that I was hard working and that I really understood it".

> I think every mistake I made was kind of like "Oh my God, they think I'm an idiot". I was terrified of that. I was terrified of being treated like I'm stupid or undeserving of being here, you know.

(Adrianna)

Like Greg, Adrianna struggled with procrastination: "I mean I survived the first year on extensions. In fact, I think I had extensions for almost every assignment". She described how she would complete assignments, "freak out over them and I wouldn't submit them" because, in her eyes, they weren't good enough.

Both Robert and Marie described how they would rather not submit an assignment at all than submit something they feared wasn't good enough.

> I kind of feel if it's not going to be perfect what's the point in doing it?
>
> (Robert)

> I didn't want to do something that wouldn't be good enough…I was so afraid of not doing it right that I couldn't do it at all.
>
> (Marie)

Marie spoke about how "I tie a lot of my self-worth into how I'm doing academically". She acknowledges that this "isn't great":

> Well, it's just a fragile thing to base it upon. You know, it's easy to do badly on an assignment, to not get the results you want. It happens. Like say in second year I got a 2:2 and everybody around me was getting firsts … I took that very badly. […] I remember, like carving 2:2 into my leg because, you know, it wasn't good enough.
>
> (Marie)

Louise, too, spoke about how her fear that an assignment was "not good enough" would prevent her from submitting it on time. She gave one example in particular where the thought of it not being good enough caused her to panic: "I just panicked … in my head I was like 'I'm gone, I'm done, I'm not going to be able to do this course'".

The pressure "to do well" was also a feature of Mai's experience: "oh my God I have to do well". She says this pressure only came about after "I got my first good grade" in her pre-university course and realised she had an opportunity to go to college. Since then she says:

> I have to do well and 90 per cent wasn't good enough, I wanted 99 per cent and if I got 99 per cent why wasn't it 100 per cent?
>
> (Mai)

Like the others before her Mai talked about how her fear that she "won't get a 1:1" has resulted in her procrastinating or, in her own words, "burying my head in the sand". She admits that "instead of actually doing a bit of study every day", she'd often "go back to bed, try not to think of it, try and fall asleep until the next day".

Joseph also describes himself as a "perfectionist – it's terrible, it's terrible". He says that in the job he had prior to returning to full-time education he was "very neat" and everything was "top quality … I'd always do a really, really good job". While he feels this is a "skill I brought to college" he also feels that it hasn't served him as well in university as it did in his manual job and instead causes him to feel "stressed".

> I would stay up till four o'clock in the morning and if I spotted one thing in my essay with syntax or a comma missing or something where the clause was wrong or something like that I would [ripping sound] four o'clock in the morning and I'd fix it.
>
> (Joseph)

Perfectionism is a complex phenomenon that has been linked to both positive (Stoeber and Otto, 2006) and negative (Lunn et al., 2023) mental health outcomes. Defined as the setting of excessively high standards for performance accompanied by overly critical self-evaluations (Frost et al., 1990), perfectionism is reportedly "adaptive", or helpful, for some and "maladaptive", or unhelpful, for others. For those whose perfectionism is described as "adaptive", it facilitates positive outcomes at university such as academic self-efficacy, self-determination, task completion, and internal locus of control (Kayis and Ceyhan, 2015) which, in turn, relate to higher exam performance and scores (Stoeber, Haskew, and Scott, 2015). For those whose perfectionism is described, in research terms, as "maladaptive", perfectionism is associated with procrastination, excessive levels of self-criticism, and emotional exhaustion. These, in turn, relate to low levels of self-worth, low mood, and high levels of anxiety (Ashby and Rice, 2002; Lunn et al., 2023).

Brown (2015, p. 130) describes perfectionism as "a self-destructive and addictive belief system that fuels this primary thought: If I look perfect and do everything perfectly, I can avoid or minimise the painful feelings of shame, judgement and blame". This belief system, and the thoughts and behaviours it fuels, was remarkably evident in the stories of the students in this book.

Upside of "it"

In spite of the difficulties presented by their distress, many students were able to recognise the positive impact this "part of me" (Marie) has had on them overall. Ella described how "it's had its downsides but it's also taught me a lot and definitely made me more compassionate, made me a lot more humble and made me a lot more willing to accept my own faults". Ella also clearly articulated the "downsides" to her anxiety and depression but says that that "focusing on the positives, it's just something you have to do because you have to focus on the positives or else you end up resenting who you are".

Kate described how

> my mum used to be "oh if I could take this away from you, if you didn't have to suffer this". Yes, there is lots of parts of this that are absolutely shit, but the people I have met, the experience it has given me, the opportunities, even if they are just so small [as] to have met such generous and kind people, yeah, it's nothing that I would ever take back.
>
> (Kate)

Kate spoke about how much and how "intensely" she has learned as a result of her experience, something that Adrianna also described. Adrianna says, "you learn from it" and that "you know things because" of the type of experiences she and the other students went through. For her there is a difference between knowing and understanding and that her life experience has left her with "a different kind of understanding". Kingsley, too, feels that "huge experiences like that change you".

> I'm a bit more wise and terrible as my experience was it really taught me a lot. In a weird way it was one of the most educational things that I have ever encountered. I mean, it has completely altered how I live and how I'm going to live for the rest of my life.
>
> (Kingsley)

Marie says, "I like what it's done to me". She feels her experience has made her "a much more empathic person" with "much more understanding" and a greater "self-awareness". Claire doesn't think she "would be the person I am today if I didn't have it". She feels it makes her a "more rational" human being and is "sure it'll stand to me in the future".

James spoke at length about how his experience has "forced" him to start "appreciating the simplest things" in life. He feels that learning to live with bipolar disorder has meant that he "can look at things a little differently to other people" and gives him a perspective on what's truly important in life. He feels this perspective and appreciation of life comes from having "been to the very bottom": "I think if you make it out the other side you've a huge advantage in life in terms of you've seen the worst of it".

Millie also described how having come through the worst of times she "can now appreciate when I have it good". She feels "the mental illness kind of taught me to look at things differently". However, while many of the students could identify the upside of "it", they also clearly acknowledged the challenges "it" presents them, particularly as they try to move on in their lives.

> Being mentally ill is difficult for me, it's difficult on my parents, it's difficult on my partner, it has a negative effect on everyone around me at one time or another.
>
> (Ella)

Conclusion

This chapter, perhaps more than any other in this book, turned away from the literature, debates, and theories surrounding the inclusion of Irish university students with mental health difficulties and, instead, turned squarely towards the experience itself. It described the nature and meaning of higher education for the students who took part in this research, charting the challenges and opportunities university represented for them personally. It delved into the day-to-day experience of students, and the routines, habits, and behaviours they have developed to manage their mental health while at university. While, as Ella suggests above, "being mentally ill is difficult", students acknowledged how this experience, and the realities that they have had to face, often at a young age, has offered them strength and resources unavailable to their peers. This "upside" to "it" is offered, not as a silver lining, but as a reflection of the balance and maturity with which students approach their distress. It is with this sense of a "whole" that we enter the final chapter.

6
Analysis, implications, and reflections

Learning objectives

1. **To analyse the key insights and reflections presented in this book** regarding the experiences, challenges, and supports available to students with mental health difficulties in Irish universities.
2. **To develop recommendations for reform for the inclusion and support of students with mental health difficulties in higher education** and identify practical ways to integrate the knowledge gained from this book into educational and professional approaches.

Introduction

This book was all about understanding. Its aim was to offer an insight into the lived experience of Irish university students with mental health difficulties so that readers might better be able to say "I understand". It began by examining what understanding is, why it is important, and how it can be garnered and developed.

Some context to the research was provided, with a particular focus on how we have understood and responded to the phenomenon of distress throughout Irish history and, more specifically, in the Irish higher education context. With orientation and context established, the body of this book was devoted to the experiences of students themselves. The transition to higher education, the provision of disability support, and the nature and meaning of higher education for students with mental health difficulties were each explored in turn.

This final chapter aims to offer some reflections based on the combination of the context (whole) of current provision for students with mental health difficulties in higher education, and the experiences (parts) shared by the 27 students who took part in this in-depth hermeneutic phenomenological research. These are simply that – reflections. They are neither conclusions nor hard "truths" but rather reflections from this particular hermeneutic cycle that may be used to inform knowledge, policy, and practice.

Supporting university students with mental health difficulties requires:

1. supporting transitions
2. re-examining the model of provision of support for students with mental health difficulties
3. financing widening participation
4. investing in people and relationships
5. celebrating and protecting the idea of a university
6. honouring the voice, experience, and wisdom of students.

1. Supporting transitions

Students with mental health difficulties are particularly vulnerable in the transition to higher education. Research suggests that students receiving treatment for their mental health are more likely to drop out of university in their first year than students not receiving mental health treatment (Zając et al., 2024). Suggested reasons for this increased attrition include "missed opportunities" at earlier stages of education, leaving students with mental health difficulties further behind upon entering university (Productivity Commission, 2020, p. 161). This, however, did not appear to be the case for the students who shared their experiences for this book. What the students in this study described was an acute sense of overwhelm and isolation which exacerbated existing vulnerabilities. Of the transition to university, Alicia said, "the whole thing was a major shock to me". John said his "mental health fell apart" and spoke of the overwhelm and self-doubt that "would come into my head 'I'm not intelligent', 'I'm not meant to be here', 'how did I get in here' [...] suicide kept crossing my mind and it came to a point where I wasn't able to do my work". Marie described how she "felt a little bit lost" while Ella said she "dropped off the grid". The common theme for all these students who really struggled in the transition to university, and even dropped out to return at a later stage, was the absence of somewhere to turn to and someone to talk to. They found support later in their university journeys, but their accounts of this vulnerable transition period are marked by a lack of preparation, support, or connection. Students who transitioned to university via the DARE, disability route were encouraged to access additional supports in their transition to higher education. These include an additional orientation session where students had an opportunity to tour the campus, get to know the disability support service and meet their disability officer or advisor. For students such as Alicia, Marie, Ella, and John, who didn't have the benefit of this additional orientation, they were significantly more vulnerable to overwhelm and dropping "off the grid" (Ella) in their first year. Ella, in particular, highlighted how the move to university, and away from the supports she had built up as a teenager, was especially detrimental. She described living away from home for the first time "with no help, trying to pretend it [her mental health difficulty] didn't exist". By January she had stopped going to university. While Ella managed to return to college the following year to begin a new course, what are notably absent from the data are the experiences of students who dropped out from university and did not return.

These experiences would suggest that all students, regardless of whether they have experienced distress, would benefit from somewhere to turn to and someone to talk to at intervals throughout their first year at university. While all students are offered some induction or orientation to their university, the stories of the students in this book remind us that transition is not something one completes in the first week or two of university but rather extends across the first year, if not further. Moreover, as was described by many students, when struggling it is often more challenging to ask for help. Scheduling one-to-one check-ins with tutors or advisors offers universities the opportunity to identify students at-risk of dropout and reduces the likelihood of a student "dropping off the grid" (Ella). Secondly, given that

15 per cent of students do not progress to their second year of university (Higher Education Authority, 2024c), the burden of paying full fees should they wish to return to higher education places a significant strain on the approximately 7,000 students who drop out each year. Given the challenges faced by all students at this critical transition point, and in particular students who struggle with their mental health, the opportunity to return to a different course, without the financial burden of full tuition fees, would be extremely beneficial for all students. Every student deserves a second chance.

2. Re-examining the model of provision of support for students with mental health difficulties

The current model of support for students with mental health difficulties in Irish universities is predicated on a disability model. This means that students with significant mental health difficulties must have a diagnosis and be classified as disabled in order to access additional support. For many students, receiving a diagnosis is a positive experience. Sophie described how "it was nice to have that feeling of validation and acknowledgement". John said he "didn't care what he [psychiatrist] said to me, you know, I just wanted him to do something for me". While, for these students, a psychiatric diagnosis offered validation and access to services such as Disability Support at university, these diagnoses are not always without repercussions. As discussed in Chapter 4, they can have long-term implications for a student's ability to secure a visa, mortgage protection, or work in certain professions. Further, for those providing support to students with mental health difficulties in higher education, there is the question of whether this model is effectively reaching the students for whom it is intended. Students who can afford to pay for a private assessment and diagnosis have the advantage of availing themselves of the benefits of the DARE scheme, such as reduced points entry to university and additional time in exams, more readily than students who have to navigate the public system with its long waiting lists and administrative delays. This inequity of access is seen in the 70 per cent of those availing of DARE who come from affluent or advantaged backgrounds (Higher Education Authority, 2024a). Given that people with disabilities are known to be at higher risk of social exclusion and deprivation (Eurostat, 2022), this proportion raises the question of whether it is time to reassess the current model of provision. This question is made all the more pressing in a climate where the numbers of students with mental health difficulties deemed eligible for disability support is increasing rapidly (rising from 643 students in 2011/2012 (AHEAD, 2012) to 3,939 in 2021/2022 (AHEAD, 2023)), and funding for higher education remains debilitatingly low (Irish Universities Association, 2023).

A universal design for learning (UDL) approach to supporting students with mental health difficulties is posited as one solution to these challenges (Healy, Banks, and Ryder, 2023). It does this by addressing the barriers to inclusive and equitable higher education at the source rather than providing "reasonable accommodations" and resources to "eligible" students to overcome these barriers later downstream. It must be noted that the students who shared their experiences as part of this book spoke highly of their university's disability support service and the support they received. They benefitted with help with "the practical stuff" (Mai) such as planning and breaking down assignments into manageable chunks but, primarily, students had the sense of reassurance of "just knowing that ... if you really do need it, there is support there" (Millie). What is clear, however, is the current model of support is under significant strain from the twin demands of increasing numbers of students and under-resourcing. It is time to reassess the current approach to including and supporting students with mental health difficulties in higher education.

3. Financing widening participation

The Irish government has relied on a highly educated workforce to realise its economic and social ambitions since the 1960s. Government initiatives such as free second level education (1967) and the "Free Fees Initiative" (1996) succeeded in widening participation to such a degree that, as of now, 80 per cent of school leavers in Ireland progress to higher education (The Irish Times, 2023). However, from the early 2000s onwards successive governments have failed to adequately fund this widening participation strategy. Student "contribution charges" were introduced and, following the economic crash in 2008, increased to €3,000, making Ireland one of the most expensive places to go to university in the European Union (Citizens Information, 2023). Simultaneously, exchequer investment in higher education has dramatically decreased. Today it is estimated that the higher education sector in Ireland is underfunded by a total of €307 million per year (Irish Universities Association, 2023). This underfunding has significant consequences at every level of the university – from lecturers on short-term precarious contracts, to high student-staff ratios, to insufficient resourcing for essential services such as disability, counselling, and learning support services, resulting in long waiting lists and session limits. Underinvestment in higher education affects everyone. It undermines the government's widening participation strategy, limits the resources available to universities to support student inclusion and engagement, and impacts individual student's ability to achieve their higher education ambitions. It is clear that the effective and meaningful inclusion of students with mental health difficulties begins with adequate resourcing.

4. Investing in people and relationships

One of the effects of under financing and under resourcing is that, as the number of students with mental health difficulties registering with university disability services increases, individual staff members are faced with larger workloads. This means that they have less time to offer each student the support they need. This is true across student services, with student counselling services reporting long waiting lists and an according limit on the number of counselling sessions they can offer students (typically 6–8) (O'Brien, 2024). Students in this book spoke so clearly about the benefit of one-to-one support. John attributes his success in college "to the people around me". Higher education, for John, presented an opportunity to move on from a past defined by "poverty", "abuse", and "deprivation". To do this, John needed support that was tailored to his individual needs. He was highly complementary of the support he received and spoke about how his one-to-one academic writing support "makes a huge difference", while his regular check in's with the campus GP offered him a consistent form of support and encouragement. John spoke about each individual without whose time and individual investment "my life would fall apart within 24 hours". He puts his successes in college "down to the people around me" as well as his own effort and determination: "I'm merely an individual that can't function without the help of other people". One-to-one interpersonal relationships with a trusted other have long been recognised as fundamental to supporting people who are struggling with their mental health (Block et al., 2022; Dooley and Fitzgerald, 2012; Dooley et al., 2019; Parker et al., 2015). These relationships require time and investment, and while it may be more cost-efficient to provide short-term automated alternatives such as mental health apps or online webinars, for those who are really struggling there is no replacement for a positive interpersonal relationship. These relationships do not always have to be professional, such as with a therapist or a disability officer. Peer support programmes have been shown to be effective for students experiencing distress (Pointon-Haas et al., 2023) as have student advisors and pastoral support (Sharp, Wray, and Maxwell, 2020). Some staff members in universities say they would benefit from specialist mental health awareness training (AHEAD, 2016), but students, when asked, speak not of the person's awareness of mental health but rather the time, patience, and generosity they are shown. Adrianna said that "being able to see someone and actually develop that relationship was one of the most important things in my life". Investing in the people, offering them the time and resources to build relationships with students in whatever their capacity, is one of the most important investments in student mental health on campus.

5. Celebrating and protecting the idea of a university

The meaning and value of higher education for students with mental health difficulties, as evidenced by the students in this book, is much greater than the sum of its credit, module, or accreditation parts. John, for example, viewed university as a way out of the abuse and deprivation of his childhood: "If you get your education nobody can take it away from you and that's why I want to get it, I want to get something that nobody can take away from me". For Leon, too, education offered him a way out of his early life circumstances. He described himself as "the black sheep" as a result of his early experience of schizophrenia. University offered him "the social acceptance of being a student" which has "helped my mental health as well, you know, because I have that social approval now". Kate described how "I feel in my life I am to learn things intently". Her anorexia nervosa had defined so much of her adolescence and early adulthood that, in returning to education, she "is trying to form a path of some type of understanding or knowledge […] I am going to see what I can learn. If over the years I have been so willing to let go of this life in an instant, well then I need to understand why I should be here". For these three students, and many others, higher education is a significant and meaningful emancipatory experience.

Irish President Michael D. Higgins (2021) suggests we are "at what I believe to be a perilous juncture in the long history of the academy". The very raison d'être of the university is under attack, according to Higgins (2021), from "market forces and the inexorable drive towards a utilitarian reductionism that is now so pervasive". This pervasiveness is seen in the closure of university arts, humanities, and social science departments (The Guardian, 2023) and the prioritisation of courses that attend to the needs of the economy (Houses of the Oireachtas, 2023) – particularly those in Science Technology Engineering and Mathematics (STEM). Citing Max Weber, Higgins (2021) described universities as "an iron cage of bureaucracy within which conformity would be demanded". Cardinal John Henry Newman (2009) in *The Idea of a University* stated that "if a practical end must be assigned to a University course, I say it is that of training good members of society". The students who shared the meaning of their experiences as part of this book further demonstrate how this "training" can be truly life-changing. In a time when the prevailing emphasis is increasingly on employability as the chief measure of a university education's value, the students in this book remind us of the purpose university has as a place to develop personal and intellectual virtues, such as curiosity, integrity, the ability and desire to seek knowledge, and to use it to be a better person and citizen. They remind us of the value of the university and how the idea of a university, as set out by Newman, Higgins, and others, needs to be celebrated and protected.

6. Honouring the voice, experience, and wisdom of students

What makes this book unique is its emphasis on the experience and knowledge of students themselves. While literature is offered to create context to the students' accounts, the voices and perspectives of students take centre stage. Policy makers, university administrators, and disability support providers are all notably absent, with their influence represented, primarily, through the students' accounts. This book was not about comprehensively analysing or explaining, but rather understanding the experience as it is lived and representing this understanding for what it is – a valuable form of knowledge. In turning to the nature of lived experience, using the book's hermeneutic phenomenological approach, the voices, experiences, and wisdom of students were brought to the fore. In doing so, this book sought to act as an example of just how valuable these experiences, this wisdom, are in developing understanding from which to develop policy or advance practice. So many of the students described how they "just want to use what I've learned to help other people" (Niamh). Engaging students, in a way that is meaningful, respectful, and protects their anonymity, is beneficial, not just for developing understanding, but for providing students with an opportunity to share the "different kind of understanding" (Adrianna) that comes with experience. Kingsley described how "huge experiences like that change you" and a mechanism to respectfully share, and openly receive, the understanding that comes through lived experience is beneficial to all.

Conclusion

Understanding, according to Heidegger (1927/1996), unfolds and develops ontologically within the hermeneutic circle. This book sought, in many ways, to emulate one hermeneutic circle. It began by exploring what we already know, the pre-understandings we hold about mental health, distress, and inclusion in higher education. These pre-understandings are themselves heavily influenced by our culture, assumptions, and our place in time and history. We then moved to the "parts" that are students' experiences of university while experiencing distress. These parts included the experience of transition to higher education; the forms of support available to, and accessed by, students, and the nature and meaning of university for students struggling with their mental health. We then moved from the parts back to the whole in the reflections of this concluding chapter. However, it does not end there. Understanding does not have a conclusion but is rather a continuous journey. The hermeneutic circle never ends. We just re-enter it from a different starting point.

Appendix
A hermeneutic phenomenological method

> Human beings, who are almost unique in having the ability to learn from the experience of others, are also remarkable for their apparent disinclination to do so.
>
> (Douglas Adams)

Introduction

One of the greatest challenges in "doing" phenomenological research, in attempting to learn from the experiences of others, is figuring out just what to "do". This appendix aims to encourage prospective hermeneutic researchers by offering, in its entirety, the method I developed to research the experiences of Irish university students with mental health difficulties presented in this book and elsewhere. It is offered in the spirit of open access, in response to the many kind emails from students and practitioners who get in touch to ask "how did you do it?". This is not the hermeneutic phenomenological method, but rather a demonstration of how one phenomenological study, beginning from a point of deep engagement with the philosophy of hermeneutic phenomenology, proceeded to understand the experiences of one cohort within the higher education system.

This approach was inspired by a desire to understand lived experience and position the experiences of others as valuable a form of knowledge as the findings from the most rigorous scientific study. To do so required attending to four inter-related commitments:

1. A commitment to the philosophical principles of hermeneutic phenomenology;
2. A commitment to the ontological and epistemological integrity of the research approach;
3. A commitment to the trustworthiness of the data and process; and
4. A commitment to ethically sensitive research.

This appendix focuses on the second, third, and fourth of these commitments. It does so with the explicit assertion that the first, an understanding of the philosophical principles of hermeneutic phenomenology, is primordial and essential. Indeed, the most frequent criticism levied at phenomenological researchers is a lack of awareness of the philosophical foundations upon which this approach to research rests. A personal understanding of the philosophy of phenomenology means that a researcher, when faced with the many inevitable day-to-day research quandaries and decisions, responds to these in a way that upholds the integrity of the approach rather than reacts with "solutions" offered by other, sometimes opposing, approaches, methodologies, or methods. The philosophy of phenomenology, and the original texts of philosophers such as Husserl, Heidegger,

Gadamer, Merleau-Ponty, and others, can initially appear intimidating and impenetrable to many, if not most, researchers. In an attempt to offer a handrail to guide first steps into this rich but often-intimidating philosophical domain, I wrote a paper, "Researching Lived Experience in Education: Misunderstood or Missed Opportunity" (Farrell, 2020), to which I brazenly refer interested researchers.

This appendix, in tun, will attend to (a) the ontological and epistemological assumptions, or paradigm, within which hermeneutic phenomenological research is conducted, (b) the method by which the data presented in this book were generated and analysed, (c) how the trustworthiness of these data were upheld and guaranteed, and (d) the measures implemented to ensure that the research was conducted and disseminated to the highest ethical standards. It will be organised by each accordingly:

1. paradigm
2. method
3. trustworthiness
4. ethical considerations.

The aspiration is to be clear and to offer practical insights into how the research was "done". Again, this is just one hermeneutic phenomenological method, offered in the hope that it might guide, encourage, and offer some sense of direction to the perspective phenomenological researcher.

1. Paradigm

Bateson (Bateson, 1972, p. 320) argued all researchers are philosophers in that "universal sense in which all human beings […]

are guided by highly abstract principles". These principles include beliefs about ontology, or the nature of reality and what can be known about it; epistemology, or the relationship between the knower and what can be known; and methodology, or how the researcher can go about finding out what they believe can be known. Thus, one's ontology directs our epistemology which in turn guides our methodology.

> The living man is bound within a net of epistemological and ontological premises which – regardless of the ultimate truth or falsity – become partially self-validating.
>
> (Bateson, 1972, p. 314)

This net, containing the researcher's ontological, epistemological, and methodological premises, is often referred to as a paradigm (Guba, 1990). A researcher's paradigm acts as a framework, or lens, through which we view a particular phenomenon. Paradigms are human constructions categorised by differences in beliefs about the nature of reality and knowledge construction. They are established by communities of scholars and as such can be neither proved nor disproved. There are a number of different research paradigms, the four major ones being positivist, postpositivist, interpretive, and critical social theory (Denzin and Lincoln, 2011).

Hermeneutic phenomenology is considered to sit within the interpretive paradigm. The interpretative paradigm evolved from the Heideggerian view of the nature of being-in-the-world and of humans as self-interpreting beings. Interpretivists study phenomena through the eyes of people in their lived situations with the ultimate goal of understanding. Benner (1994) highlights how interpretive inquiry is concerned with articulating, appreciating, and making visible the voices, concerns, and practices of those who are the focus of the inquiry.

The interpretive paradigms assumes a relative ontology (there are multiple realities), a subjectivist epistemology (knower and respondent co-create understandings), and a naturalistic (in the natural world) set of methodologies (Denzin and Lincoln, 2011). Ontologically, the interpretive paradigm is based on relativism, a view of truth as composed of multiple realities that can only be subjectively perceived. Epistemologically, interpretivists believe that knowledge is subjective; that there is no one ultimate or "correct" way of knowing. This epistemological view of knowledge as subjective has led some to consider interpretivism a paradox in that interpretivists attempt to develop an objective science from subjective experience (Denzin and Lincoln, 2011). Rainbow and Sullivan (1987) attest that this paradox is based on an objective-subjective split when, in fact, as Munhall (2012) points out, "objectivity is a subjective notion".

Methodologies associated with the interpretive paradigm, reflecting both its relativist ontology and subjective epistemology, are united by an emphasis on the intersubjective construction of meaning and understanding. Knowledge is generated in interpretive research when "relevant insights emerge naturally through research-participant discourse" (Coffey and Atkinson, 1996, p. 54). Therefore, the researcher's perspective is inextricably bound up within the findings of an interpretive inquiry. The interpretive paradigm views knowledge building as an inherently social act (the hermeneutic circle) and, as a result, methodologies within this paradigm tend to be qualitative.

While methodology (stemming from the Greek *hodos* meaning "way" and logos meaning "to study") refers to "the pursuit of knowledge", method (stemming from the Greek *methodos*) refers to the "mode" by which knowledge is pursued. The mode by which knowledge was pursued in this study forms the focus of the next section.

2. Method

> Some people speak of a method greedily, demandingly; what they want in work is method; to them it never seems rigorous enough, formal enough. Method becomes a Law … the invariable fact is that a work which constantly proclaims its will-to-method is ultimately sterile … [there is] no surer way to kill a piece of research and send it to join the great scrap heap of abandoned projects than Method.
>
> (Barthes, 1986, p. 318)

Heidegger talked about phenomenological reflection as following certain woodland paths towards a "clearing" where something could be shown or revealed in its essential nature. These paths (*methodos*), however, cannot be determined by fixed signposts, rather "they need to be discovered or invented as a response to the question at hand" (van Manen, 1990, p. 29). Indeed, it has been said that the method of hermeneutic phenomenology is that there is no method (Gadamer, 1979; Rorty, 1979).

What is offered here is the *methodos* by which the experiences of the students represented throughout this book were generated, analysed, and understood. It is not the method of hermeneutic phenomenology by any means, but just one method that might offer insights and points of reflection for other hermeneutic phenomenological researchers. I hope it is helpful.

2.1 Research questions

The methodological point of departure for any study is its research question(s). These are especially important in hermeneutic phenomenological research where, in the necessary absence of a clearly delineated set of directions, they offer a guiding and welcome picture of the destination. Returning to these research questions, to this image of the destination, at regular intervals throughout the research journey helps ensure that the research stays on track.

This study was underpinned by two research questions:

1. What is the nature of the lived experience of students with mental health difficulties in higher education?
2. What meaning do these students ascribe to their experience?

Once established, these research questions also helped determine the what (nature and meaning of mental health difficulties), the who (university students with mental health difficulties), and the how (data generation and analysis) of the study. Each of these will be examined in turn, beginning with the sample (the what and the who) before turning to the method of data generation and analysis (the how).

2.2 Sample
Sampling

According to Steeves (Steeves, 2000, p. 45), sampling "implies that a researcher is choosing informants because those informants might have something to say about an experience they share with others". As a result, qualitative researchers typically, although not exclusively, employ non-probability sampling techniques. Non-probability sampling refers to a number of sampling strategies (e.g. convenience sampling, purposive sampling, opportunistic sampling, quota sampling, judgemental sampling, and snowball sampling). Non-probability sampling techniques, in contrast to probability sampling (the word probability deriving from the Latin *probabilitas*, a measure of authority or authoritativeness), do not aim to generate a sample representative of the entire population. Herein lies what many consider the major weakness of non-probability sampling.

> Basically, non-probability samples are not samples at all but could be regarded as complete populations from which no statistical generalisations to larger populations can be made.
>
> (Abdellah and Levine, 1979, p. 332)

However, as the aim of qualitative research is to generate rich, contextually laden, explanatory data, it has little concern with generalisations or generating population-based estimates. Indeed, the relevance of generalisability to qualitative research has long been disputed, with transferability deemed a more appropriate measure of probabilitas (Lincoln and Guba, 1985; Sandelowski, 1986). Research subjects in qualitative studies are selected, not because they increase the study's p-value, but because they provide insight into the phenomenon under study.

Purposive sampling was the non-probability sampling strategy adopted for this study. Purposive sampling is based on the premise that study participants should be chosen based on the purpose of their involvement in the study. The strength and potency of purposive sampling, argues Quinn Patton (2002, p. 230), "lie in selecting information-rich cases for study in-depth […] those [cases] from which one can learn a great deal about issues of central importance to the purpose of the inquiry". As the purpose of this study was to explore the lived experience of distress, direct experience of a mental health difficulty was an essential criterion for participation. The type or severity of mental health problem was not pertinent, nor was "expert" (e.g. psychiatrist or other mental health professional) validation or diagnosis. Hermeneutic phenomenology aims to understand subjective experience, and as distress is a highly subjective experience, it was considered futile to attempt to objectively categorise (i.e. via diagnoses, psychiatric classifications) this experience. However, by virtue of the majority of participants being recruited through university disability services, which, as discussed in Chapters 2 and 4, require a diagnosis as evidence of eligibility, the majority of the students in this study had received a diagnosis.

Sample size

Sample size is often one of the most perplexing issues in hermeneutic phenomenological research. When Harry Wolcott (1994,

p. 3) was asked "how many qualitative interviews is enough?" by a team of researchers from the British National Centre for Research Methods, he replied "the answer, as with all things qualitative, is 'it depends'". Phenomenological studies, however, tend to involve smaller sample sizes as these are more cost and time efficient and allow for greater focus on depth rather than breadth. Speaking about sample size, Quinn Patton suggests:

> No rule of thumb exists to tell a researcher precisely how to focus a study. The extent to which a research or evaluation study is broad or narrow depends on purpose, the resources available, the time available, and the interests of those involved. In brief, these are not choices between good and bad but choices among alternatives, all of which have merit.
>
> (Quinn Patton, 2002, p. 228)

This research began with an anticipated sample size of 10–12 students. However, when an invitation was extended through three recruitment channels (youth mental health service and two university disability support services) the level of interest from students far exceeded expectations. It became clear that the opportunity to share their story rather than be "subjected" to a researcher-defined battery of questions, or survey, was of great interest to students. It was decided that, in line with the "open" principle of hermeneutic phenomenology, all students who would like to share their experiences should be offered the opportunity to participate (even if it did add a year to the research!). In total, 27 students shared their experiences as part of this study (Table 1).

Table 1 Participants – Overview

Pseudonym	Age	Sex	UG/PG	Field of study*	Interviews
Adrianna	22	F	UG	AHSS	2
Alicia	22	F	UG	AHSS	1
Annie	21	F	UG	AHSS	2
Ashley	22	F	UG	AHSS	1
Claire	20	F	UG	STEM	1
Ella	21	F	UG	AHSS	1
Faye	20	F	UG	Health Sciences	1
Fiona	19	F	UG	AHSS	1
Greg	29	M	PG	STEM	1
J. D.	20	M	UG	AHSS	1
James	26	M	PG	STEM	1
John	29	M	UG	AHSS	1
Joseph	43	M	UG	AHSS	1
Kate	27	F	PG	AHSS	1
Kinsley	21	M	UG	AHSS	1
Lauren	21	F	UG	AHSS	1
Leon	41	M	UG	AHSS	1
Louise	30	F	UG	Health Sciences	2
Mai	22	F	UG	Health Sciences	1
Marie	23	F	UG	STEM	2
Mary	26	F	PG	AHSS	2
Millie	19	F	UG	AHSS	1
Niamh	21	F	PG	AHSS	1

Pseudonym	Age	Sex	UG/PG	Field of study*	Interviews
Robert	25	M	UG	AHSS	1
Sarah	26	F	PG	AHSS	2
Sophie	20	F	UG	AHSS	2
Thomas	19	M	UG	AHSS	2

Legend:

UG – Undergraduate

PG – Postgraduate

AHSS – Arts, Humanities, and Social Sciences

STEM – Science, Technology, Engineering, and Mathematics

* – Students were grouped broadly under one of the three major departments adopted by most major Irish universities. This was so as to provide insight into the student's area of study without providing overly specific detail that might reveal their identity.

2.3 Data generation

> The genuine will to know calls for the spirit of generosity rather than for that of economy, for reverence rather than for subjugation, for the lens rather than for the hammer.
>
> (Spiegelberg, 1984, p. 680)

Data, stemming from the Latin *datum* meaning something "given" or "granted", reflects the manner in which a hermeneutic phenomenological researcher is "given" an insight into another's experience. However, as van Manen (1990) points out, experiential accounts are never identical to the lived experiences, rather transformations of those experiences:

> So the upshot is that we need to find access to life's living dimensions while realising that the meanings we bring to the surface from the depths of life's oceans have already lost the natural quiver of their undisturbed existence.
>
> (van Manen, 1990, p. 54)

The point of hermeneutic phenomenological data generation is to "borrow" other people's experiences in order to form an understanding of the deeper meaning of an aspect of human experience. The data of other people's experiences allows us to become more informed, shaped, and enriched, enabling us to render a fuller understanding of the phenomena in question. Hermeneutic phenomenological data may be generated using a number of techniques. These include conversational interviewing, eliciting written responses, participation observation, and oral or written biographies. However, the most commonly employed data generation technique in hermeneutic phenomenological research is conversational interviewing. Conversational interviewing is an effective means of exploring and gathering experiential narrative material with the aim of developing a richer and deeper understanding of a human phenomenon (van Manen, 1990). The conversational nature of hermeneutic phenomenological interviewing allows for what Bernstein (1991, p. 4) calls the "to-and-fro play of dialogue" with the ultimate aim of a "fusion of horizons'"(Gadamer, 1960/1989) between researcher and participant.

A total of 35 conversational interviews were carried out with 27 students. These ranged in duration from 40 minutes (for a second interview) to 90 minutes, with an average of just over an hour. Those students who expressed interest in participating were provided with detailed information about the study and the opportunity to ask any questions that they might have. At this stage, if the student was happy to proceed, a date and time for the first interview was arranged. The student was met in a public place and walked to a quiet room in which the interview was to take place. This offered an opportunity to chat to the student more informally and, hopefully, put them at ease, plus overcome the intimidating prospect of expecting the student to find a small, third-floor room in a large, unfamiliar building. Once settled in the quiet interview room, the aims of the study would be reiterated, with a particular emphasis on how the study was very much about understanding the student's experience, that there were no right or wrong answers, and that what was important was whatever was important to the student themselves. The consent form was discussed and the students invited to ask any questions before signing the consent form. At this point the digital recorder was turned on.

Each interview was guided by just one question – can you tell me a little about yourself and your experience? From here the student would typically begin by describing themselves, what they were studying and a little about their family/living situation. However, often within the first five minutes, the student would begin to settle in, open up, and share their story – the story of their experience of "it" (whatever "it" happened to be). Interviews typically lasted between 60 and 90 minutes, with most conversations drawing to a close naturally at about the 60-minute mark. It was my responsibility, as researcher, to guide the student back – re-orienting them to the present by asking about their plans for the rest of the day or chatting casually about upcoming assignments or plans for mid-term break. It was an opportunity to check in and ask how they were after our conversation and reiterate the support available to them by virtue of participation in the study, if they needed it. Directly after the interview, I would make notes in the field journal. These would often be added to later in the day, and sometimes in the days following the interview, as new thoughts, ideas, and reflections came to mind.

A follow-up email was sent to every student the evening after their interview. Each was personalised, expressing the appreciation and enormous respect felt towards the participant. It was outlined that, sometimes after going back over such deeply personal issues, the student might feel vulnerable and, if they were at all concerned, the student was encouraged to get in touch and additional support could be provided if necessary. For students who only did one interview, they were invited to stay in touch and were reminded that they would be updated about the research at various points throughout its life course. For students taking part in a second interview, the process above was repeated a second time

The conversational interviews themselves were just that – conversational. The experience, as researcher, of walking into a room to meet a stranger without an interview schedule or any sense of how things were going to unfold, was intimidating, to say the least. It offered a sense of how reassuring a clipboard with a series of guiding questions could be and how, particularly during the first few interviews, a lack of clear structure meant that every interview was a journey into the great unknown. However, the lack of structure proved to be one of this approach's greatest offerings in that it created space for the student to take the researcher through their experiences, thoughts, and feelings without these being curtailed or restricted by the pre-ordained conventions of an interview schedule or hypothesis-driven agenda.

My task as research was to simply initiate the conversation with the question above (can you tell me a little about yourself and your experience?) and interject only when (a) I didn't quite understand something and needed clarification, (b) when trains of thought or conversation slowed or appeared to come to a halt and needed to be restarted and, (c) from time to time, to gently steer the focus back to what it was actually like (lived experience) and rather than getting overly caught up in the "and then this happened". Prior to almost every interview I was worried that, without the handrail of a series of pre-prepared questions, the conversation would fall flat. However, time and again I was astonished at how much students wanted to share, and how much they thrived upon the opportunity to tell their story in their own words, in their own way, and in their own time. The richness and complexity captured in the data presented in this book and in other publications from this research bears testimony to this.

The check-in emails sent to each student after every interview had a two-fold intent – to thank them for giving so much during the interview and to check that it hadn't taken too much out of them or brought any difficult feelings or memories back to the surface. However, it also offered them an opportunity to feed back, not only how they were doing, but how they found the experience overall. The following feedback, offered by Niamh, reflected the student's appreciation not only of the approach and its value in informing responses to mental health issues, but the opportunity to be empathically and respectfully listened to.

> I haven't really ever opened up or talked in depth about those experiences since therapy a few years ago. It was incredibly emotional for me I guess but a huge satisfaction came from it especially today I feel like a weight off my shoulders. It's an honour to talk to someone so incredibly empathetic and a great listener and I hope it will help your research and it will future allow other professionals in the mental health care services that peoples experiences have such a huge richness and so much can come from it. I admire the approach you have taken and the time and effort it takes.
>
> (Niamh, in response to check-in email)

A total of 36 hours of audio was recorded over the course of the 35 conversational interviews, and this yielded, when transcribed verbatim, 997 pages of written data. The next step was to analyse these data.

2.4 Data analysis

Perhaps the greatest challenge in adopting a philosophical approach such as hermeneutic phenomenology is translating its often complex philosophical concepts into methodological techniques. Indeed, as Roberts and Taylor (1998, p. 109) have noted, "many of the so-called phenomenological methods leave prospective researchers wondering just what to do". In attempting to overcome this challenge, data generated over the course of this study were analysed using a combination of the principles of the hermeneutic circle and the methodological framework for thematic analysis offered by Braun and Clarke (2006).

The hermeneutic circle as method of interpretation

The concept of the hermeneutic circle can be viewed from both ontological and methodological perspectives. Heidegger and Gadamer both viewed the circularity of interpretation not so much as a methodological principle, but as a ubiquitous and inescapable feature of all human efforts to understand. As such there is no method, experience, or meaning that is independent of the hermeneutic circle. Moreover, all efforts to interpret or understand are always located within some background (e.g. socio-historical tradition, value system, or practice) that cannot be ignored. Prior to generating and analysing the data, time was devoted to explicating this background (a significantly abridged version of this explication can be seen in Chapters 1 and 2).

The hermeneutic circle is essentially based on the idea that understanding the meaning of a text as a whole involves making sense of the parts, and grasping the meaning of the parts depends on having some sense of the whole. As such, interpretive understanding goes forward in stages, with continual movement between the parts and the whole allowing understanding to be enlarged and deepened.

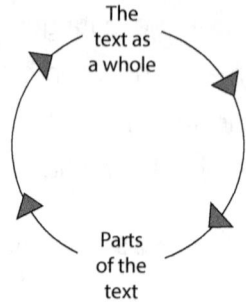

Figure 1 The hermeneutic circle as method of interpretation.

The hermeneutic circle, by its very circular nature, suggests that the meaning of a text is not something that can grasped once and for all. Meaning exists in a complex interplay between parts and whole. Braun and Clarke's (2006) six-step process of data analysis provided a flexible framework for analysing the "parts" as well as the "whole" of the text. It is a framework that enjoys "theoretical freedom" (Braun and Clarke, 2006, p. 5) in that it is applicable across a range of epistemological and theoretical approaches without impeding on the particular values of an approach such as hermeneutic phenomenology. As Braun and Clarke (2006, p. 4) themselves acknowledge, "one of the benefits of thematic analysis is its flexibility". As such, it is a methodological framework that can be adapted to align more closely with the approach taken. Figure 2 outlines the relationship between the data analysis procedure employed in this study, Braun and Clarke's (2006) method of thematic analysis, and the hermeneutic circle itself.

Appendix 117

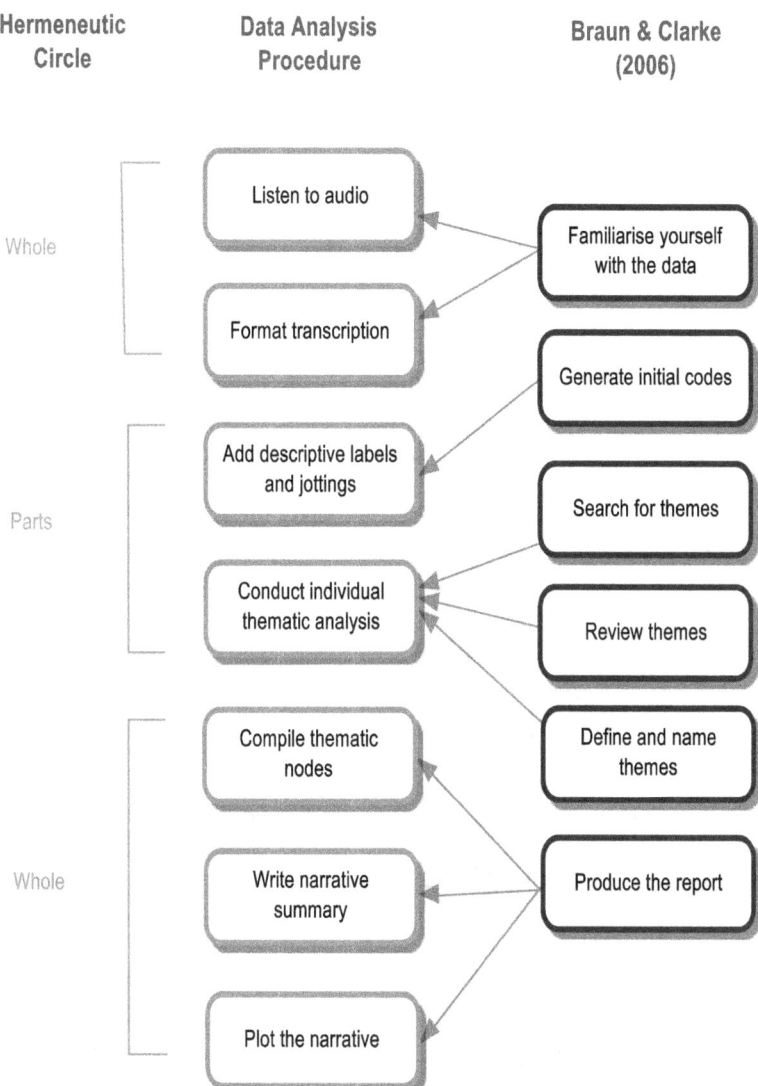

Figure 2 Relationship between individual data analysis procedure, hermeneutic circle and Braun and Clarke's (2006) method of thematic analysis.

The steps taken to analyse the data in this study were as follows.

1. **Listen to audio**. Each interview was listened to and transcribed verbatim.
2. **Format transcription**. Each interview was listened to a second time, checked for accuracy, and the transcripts formatted for analysis. This simply involved coping the data from the masterfile into a new document, increasing the line spacing and adding a wide margin on one side for the descriptive labels and jottings below.
3. **Add descriptive labels and jottings**. Each interview was listened to for a third time and descriptive labels and jottings were added to a margin constructed along the side of the transcript. This was the point at which content and themes began to be noted and a sense of what the dataset reveals overall began to form. The labels and jottings at this stage mainly comprised striking quotations or words used by the students. This helped ensure the labelling process remained as true to the students' own words as possible.
4. **Conduct individual thematic analysis**. Each individual student's data set was analysed thematically. This step enveloped three of Braun and Clarke's methodological steps (as seen in Figure 2). It also marked the step where the data began to be "transformed" (Wolcott, 1994). This transformation involved actively uncovering themes or, as van Manen (1990, p. 90) describes them, "knots in the webs of our experiences, around which certain lived experiences are spun and thus lived through as meaningful wholes". A theme, according to Braun and Clarke (2006, p. 82), "captures something important about the data in relation to the research question, and represents some level of patterned response

or meaning within the data set". This individual level of analysis continued for each student and, once completed, was followed by a "stepping back" and taking stock of all of the themes or thematic nodes generated.

5. **Compile thematic nodes**. Each of the 331 thematic nodes generated by phases 1–4 was written on individual strips of card with the student's pseudonym written on the back. Each piece of card was then laid out, organised, and collapsed under thematic headings. For example, "'picked on' by teachers" (Mai), "Bullying" (Marie, Ella, Niamh, J. D., Sophie), and "Dyslexia" (J. D., Sarah) were all themes relating to issues that students described affecting their early school experiences and so were collapsed under the thematic heading of "Difficulties in School". Significant time and thought were dedicated to this organising and compiling, and the sounding board of a "critical friend" (see trustworthiness section below) was particularly helpful in this process.

6. **Write the narrative summary** offered the opportunity to step back and review the "whole". It involved writing a "narrative summary" of each student's story that was both temporal and thematic, that is, it told their story, as they described it unfolding, and ensured that the major themes identified in earlier phases were represented in this chronological telling. The anonymised narrative summaries of each of the 27 participants were presented as an appendix in the final report. During the data generation process, and particularly in the early stages of data analysis, a structure began to emerge from the students' narratives. It became clear that the students themselves, when given freedom and space to tell their story in their own words, did so in a particular way. Their

stories followed a "plot". Step seven involved plotting this narrative for each student.

7. **Plot the narrative.** While the plotting of the initial stories began as an exercise in curiosity, it became clear that this structure was revealing something very important about the way in which the students were making sense of their experiences. It revealed the narrative meaning that the students had ascribed to their experiences and, as the same structure emerged in dataset after dataset, the plotting of narrative became not only an integral part of the data analysis process but a unique way of viewing each dataset, both in terms of its "parts" and its "whole". These plots can be seen in Farrell (2022b).

This process of analysis yielded:

1. 27 narrative summaries
2. 46 themes (i.e. the nature of the lived experience)
3. A four-phase plot which offered an insight into how students organised their experiences into meaningful wholes (i.e. meaning).

At every stage of the research process, measures were taken to uphold the validity or trustworthiness of the data and to ensure that the research was conducted to the highest ethical standards. These measures form the focus of the remainder of this methodological appendix.

3. Trustworthiness

Up until the late twentieth century, social science researchers had developed a certain degree of consensus about what counted as knowledge and, more importantly, what kind of knowledge claims could be validated. However, the "narrative turn", which occurred towards the end of the century, posited a challenge to conventional forms of evidence. Researchers steering the narrative turn, which Polkinghorne (2007, p. 472) collectively refers to as "reformists", argued that personal descriptions of life experiences offered knowledge about important, but often neglected, aspects of the human realm. The pre-existing group, which Polkinghorne (2007, p. 472) refers to as "conventionalists", struggled to accept this new movement. Their dismissal of the claims generated by this form of research was largely justified by the failure of the claims to withstand conventional measures of validity.

> Typically, the issue of validity is approached by applying one's own community's protocols about what, in its view, is acceptable evidence and appropriate analysis to the other community's research. In these cases the usual conclusion is that the other community's research is lacking in support for its knowledge claims.
>
> (Polkinghorne, 2007, p. 474)

In response, researchers, such as Lincoln and Guba (1985), took conventional criteria for establishing the "trustworthiness" of claims and developed parallel criteria for more qualitative research approaches. These criteria of credibility, transferability, dependability, and confirmability will structure the discussion around this study's efforts to uphold standards of rigour and trustworthiness. Table 2 provides a visual overview of conventional measures of validity, Lincoln and Guba's (Lincoln and Guba, 1985) parallel criteria for qualitative research, and the measures taken to uphold and demonstrate efforts to ensure that the data,

Table 2 Criteria for establishing trustworthiness (Lincoln and Guba, 1985) and measures taken to ensure trustworthiness in this study

	Scientific paradigm criteria	Lincoln and Guba (1985)	Measures taken
Truth values	Internal validity	Credibility	✓ "Phenomenological nod" ✓ Critical friend ✓ Field journal
Applicability	External validity	Transferability	✓ Narrative summaries ✓ Sample transcript and analysed outputs from this transcript ✓ Critical friend
Consistency Neutrality	Reliability Objectivity	Dependability Confirmability	✓ Overview of approach taken ✓ Explication of researcher's bias ✓ Outline of methodology

Scientific paradigm criteria	Lincoln and Guba (1985)	Measures taken
		✓ Audit trail
		✓ Direct quotations
		✓ Critical friend report
		✓ Sample transcript and analysed outputs from this transcript

interpretations, and claims espoused in this study are, in so far as it is possible, trustworthy.

3.1 Credibility

The term "credibility" is used to represent the truth value of the research. Lincoln and Guba (1985) claim that a study is credible when it presents such faithful descriptions that when co-researchers or readers are confronted with the interview transcriptions they recognise the thematic conclusions. The Dutch phenomenologist Buytendijk referred to the "phenomenological nod" as a way of indicating that a credible phenomenological description is something we can nod to, recognising it as an experience that we have had or could have had (van Manen, 1990). In order to ensure that all conclusions arrived at in the current research are firmly grounded in the data, a random selection (n=4) of interviews – their recordings, transcripts, thematic analyses, narrative summaries, and plots – were read and assessed by a "critical friend". With a background in philosophical criticality, the critical friend was well poised to assess the credibility and truth value of the data analysis. According to Koch (1994), credibility in hermeneutic phenomenology is enhanced when researchers describe and interpret their experience as researchers. She believes self-awareness to be essential and recommends researchers keep a journal "in which the content and process of interactions are noted, including reactions to various events" (Koch, 1994, p. 92). A detailed field journal was maintained throughout the data generation, analysis, and "write up" phases of this research project. Comprising of two full Moleskine notebooks, the field journal(s) offered a space to record details around the data generation process, my own reflection on the experience of engaging in the "to-and-fro" of each conversational interview, and any instances my own pre-judgements or prejudice may have bubbled to the surface. It also offered a space to consider the identification of themes in the analysis process and the many factors that may have resulted in "seeing" some themes and not others.

3.2 Transferability

The applicability of conventional social science research is assessed by how well threats to external validity have been managed. These threats include anything that may interfere with a study's ability to produce claims about cause-and-effect relationships that are generalisable to populations. Reformist approaches, in contrast, believe generalisability itself to be somewhat of an illusion and focus, not on cause-and-effect relationships, but on understanding human experiences. Guba and Lincoln (1985) suggest that the applicability of such research is better established by its transferability or "fittingness" into similar contexts.

> A study meets the criterion of fittingness when its findings can "fit" into contexts outside the study situation and when its audience views its findings as meaningful and applicable in terms of their own experiences. In addition the findings of the study, whether in the form of description, explanation, or theory, "fit" the data from which they are derived.
>
> (Sandelowski, 1986, p. 32)

Contextual information is essential if a reader is to assess whether findings "fit" into particular contexts. Accordingly, the reader was provided a detailed narrative summary which provided contextual information, not only on the student and their story, but on the process by which the story was generated and analysed. Moreover, a full transcript was provided so that the reader was able to read a verbatim account of an interview and determine if the interpretations of this data, presented in the narrative summary and in the findings relating to that particular student, "fit" with the data from which they are drawn. The critical friend had an opportunity to do this with four full transcripts and their appraisal of transferability was included in the final report.

3.3 Dependability and confirmability

> There is no neutrality. There is only greater or less awareness of one's biases.
>
> (Rose, 1985, p. 77)

The consistency and neutrality of an inquiry, sometimes spoken of in terms of "reliability" and "objectivity", refer to the degree to which various readers or researchers may arrive at comparable, but not contradictory, conclusions given the same data (dependability), as well as the degree to which the conclusions may be confirmed by the data (confirmability). Lincoln and Guba (1985) suggest that both dependability and confirmability are best assessed based on the study's "auditability".

> Essentially an auditor called in to authenticate the accounts of a business or industry is expected to perform two tasks. First, he or she examines the process by which the accounts were kept, to satisfy stakeholders that they are not the victims of what is sometimes called "creative accounting" [...]. The second task of the auditor is to examine the product – the records – from the point of view of their accuracy.
>
> (Lincoln and Guba, 1985, p. 318)

Just as a fiscal auditor should have access to details of the process, the inquiry auditor, or reader, should have access to the details of the process by which the product – the data, findings, interpretations, and claims – was developed. The final report included details of the approach itself, an exposition of my own prejudice, as well as an audit trail detailing the sampling strategy and data generation and analysis processes. The reader was also offered an opportunity to examine the accuracy of the "product" in a number of ways. These included (a) the use of direct quotations, complete with reference to the page of transcript from which they were taken, (b) the critical friend report which provided an outsider assessment of the dependability and confirmability of four, randomly selected, transcripts and their outputs, and (c) access to one complete transcript, its initial analysis, the thematic conclusions drawn, and the manner in which the student's story was "plotted" onto the narrative structure than emerged in the study.

In being able to assess the process of the inquiry, the reader was able to attest to its dependability (Table 2). Equally, in examining the product, the reader was able to confirm the degree to which the product is supported by the data. As such, auditability offers a means of assessing both the dependability and confirmablity of the study (Lincoln and Guba, 1985). Research cannot be considered trustworthy, that is, credible, transferable, dependable, and confirmable, unless it is, in the first instance, ethical.

4. Ethical considerations

Hermeneutic phenomenological research methods, such as conversational interviewing, typically require the researcher to enter the participant's lifeworld and access their lived experience (Polit and Hungler, 1999). This intrusion into the private sphere means that hermeneutic phenomenological research is categorised as "sensitive" research. Consequently, ethical considerations are of great importance in research adopting a hermeneutic phenomenological approach, particularly this study which sought to access the lived experience of psychological distress. Gaining ethical approval is at the heart of all research, particularly sensitive research. Accordingly, this study necessitated, and was successfully awarded, ethical approval from the ethics committees of the two universities and one mental health service from which students were recruited.

This research was underpinned by two main ethical principles: informed consent and confidentiality.

1. **Informed consent** is the principle that participants should not be coerced or pressured into research against their will, but that their participation should be based on voluntarism and with full understanding of the implications of participation. Informed consent has been the cornerstone of ethical guidelines since the Nuremberg Code – a code established as a result of the atrocities carried out by medical professionals during the Second World War. Students who volunteered to participate in this study were informed about the aims of this research, what participation would entail, and their rights as participants in a number of ways. They were provided with a copy of the consent form and given time to read this in advance of the initial interview. The interview itself began with a verbal reiteration of the study's aims and the students' rights, as well as an opportunity to ask any questions, before the student completed and signed the informed consent form.

2. **Confidentiality**: The Declaration of Helsinki which outlines the ethical principles of medical research, added confidentiality and privacy to the Nuremberg Code. Confidentiality means not disclosing information gained from research in other settings, such as everyday informal conversation. It also relates to the protection of the identity of participants and sites in published accounts of the research. Participant confidentiality was a significant factor in this study – one that was taken very seriously. The only instance in which

confidentiality would have been breached was in the event that participants were deemed to be at immediate risk of harming themselves or others. This was in line with standard ethical practice in mental health research (Psychological Society of Ireland, 2011) and participants were made fully aware of this limit to confidentiality verbally, in the information sheet and in the consent form which they were asked to sign before the first interview. Thankfully, this did not emerge as an issue at any stage throughout the study but if it had a protocol was in place at all times to ensure the researcher could access additional supports for the students if necessary. Anonymity was an important aspect of confidentiality. Students were asked to choose their own pseudonym – a name that they liked and felt represented them without making them in any way identifiable. Other distinguishing features such as names, places, courses of study, or events that would be considered usual or likely to make the student identifiable were altered to protect the student's identity.

In addition to these two cornerstones of ethical research, Beauchamp and Childers (2001) outline a number of moral principles upon which ethical research practice is based. These are:

Respect for autonomy: respecting an individual's right to make decisions and enabling them to make reasoned informed choices.

Respect for autonomy means respecting the participants' freedom to decide what to do. This particularly relates to the students' right to withdraw at any time without having to offer a reason. As already outlined, students were informed about their rights as participants in a number of ways – the participant information sheet, verbally at their first interview, and again in the consent form where they were required to tick boxes to confirm that they understood what was being asked of them and their rights as participants (including the right to withdraw at any time without giving a reason). Moreover, respect was one of the strongest values underpinning this research and respect for the student, and the stories they shared, extended far beyond the data generation process to every aspect of the analysis, write up, and dissemination phases.

Beneficence: seeking to achieve the best balance between risk and benefit that achieves the greatest benefits for the individual.

This study sought to capture the unique insight and expertise of those with lived experience of psychological distress so as to better understand the experience. At the outset, it wasn't clear whether the participant would see any personal benefit in participating in the study. In addition, there was concern that participation might result in the student revisiting painful experience which may be distressing for them. However, as the data generation process unfolded it became clear that participating in this research offered students a rare opportunity to be listened to; to be truly heard for what they had to say without being interrupted or corrected; and for their perspectives and insights to be held as valuable sources of knowledge. In addition, students spoke about how much they wished to share their experiences in the hope that it might one day help someone else in a similar situation. It appears that these two, largely unforeseen, aspects of participation meant that sharing their stories as part of the research was a worthwhile and even "cathartic" (Kinsley – follow-up email) experience for the students.

> I would feel so happy if I could help even one person out there to avoid the mistakes I made growing up … I was unlucky but through modern research I'm hoping that other people do not have to suffer like I did.
>
> (Joseph)

Justice: addressing issues fairly for individuals in the same or similar situation.

This study viewed the phenomenon of psychological distress, to borrow Marcel's (1950) sentiment, not as a problem in need of a solution but a mystery in need of evocative comprehension. It does not seek justice or to unravel a problem, rather to achieve a direct contact with the world of living with psychological distress. In this sense, the present study sought to "do justice" to participants' lived experiences rather than result in justice for participants and those in a similar situation.

Non-maleficence: avoiding causing harm.

The protection of those who participated in this study was of utmost concern. This concern extended beyond the important ethical aspects associated with the data generation process, to the protection of the students accounts, and the integrity with which these stories were treated during analysis, presentation, and dissemination.

Conclusion

The ability to learn from the experiences of others, as Adams suggests at the beginning of this appendix, presents one of the greatest opportunities available to us as human beings. Hermeneutic phenomenology represents a powerful way of understanding lived experience. However, many prospective hermeneutic phenomenological researchers struggle to find an entry point into the complex philosophy of phenomenology; to align the ontological, epistemological, and methodological orientations of the approach; to demonstrate the trustworthiness or validity of the research; and to know that they have considered all possible ethical requirements. I hope that prospective hermeneutic phenomenological researchers will be reassured, even encouraged, in reviewing this one attempt to research lived experience. I wish you well.

Recommended assignments

Chapter 1
Questions for discussion:
1. Should we consider lived experience as a form of evidence? If so, why? If not, why not?
2. Why have we come to value other forms of knowledge more than our own experience?
3. What is the relationship between power and what we consider trustworthy/evidence?
4. What does the language we use to describe and re-present a phenomenon such as distress or mental illness tell us about our interpretations/understandings of the phenomenon?

Chapter 2
"We want a truly inclusive third level system where neither your background nor experience has a bearing on your ability to attend or succeed in higher education." – Minister for Further and Higher Education Simon Harris at the launch of the National Access Plan (2022) 31st of August 2022.

1. What are the implications of this statement for students? For society? For universities? For government?

2. What are the opportunities and costs of widening participation in higher education?
3. What is the purpose of higher education?
4. What are the strengths and limitations of a disability approach to the inclusion of students with mental health difficulties in higher education?

Chapter 3
Questions for discussion

1. What is a transition? Is it a short (2-3 week) period as one enters a university? Or is it a more personal journey that spans the many transition points into, within, and out of higher education?

Reflection

Reflect on your own experience of transition to higher education. What helped you in this transition? What challenges did you experience? What would have helped you overcome these challenges? How might the transition experiences of students with mental health difficulties differ? Drawing on the experiences of the students in this book, how might these students be better supported in the transition to higher education?

Chapter 4
Questions for discussion

1. What are the opportunities and implications of diagnosis for students with mental health difficulties?

2. Is mental health/mental illness a disability?
3. What, from the accounts of students shared in this book, were the most helpful aspects of disability support? In what way do you think these were helpful?
4. "Fitness to Practise means having the necessary skills, knowledge, health, personal resilience and ongoing appropriate conduct and dispositions to undertake and complete, safely and effectively, a programme that includes elements of professional practice, experiential learning or clinical work."

Only professionals who meet Fitness to Practise requirements should be allowed to work in health and social care professions – Discuss.

Chapter 5
Questions for discussion

1. What are the day-to-day challenges experienced by university students with mental health difficulties? How might these be overcome – by universities; student support services; the student themselves?
2. What is perfectionism? Are students with mental health difficulties more likely to experience perfectionism? Or is perfectionism more likely to lead to distress?

Chapter 6
Activity

1. Develop a series of recommendations for the inclusion and support of students with mental health difficulties in higher

education – for Government; for Universities; for student support services; for lecturers/tutors; for students.

2. Identify three ways in which the student experiences and learning from the book will influence your current/future practice.

Notes

Chapter 3 Transition to higher education

1. In so far as possible, the words, terms and diagnoses that the students used will be represented in this book. This is done to honour the language and meaning of the students themselves. For example, Leon spoke about having "paranoid schizophrenia" – a term that is no longer recognised by professionals and was removed from the American Psychiatric Association's Diagnostic and Statistical Manual of Mental Disorders Fifth Edition (DSM-5) in 2013 and the World Health Organisation's International Classification of Diseases when updating to its 11th edition in 2019. As described in chapters one and two, the professional and cultural understanding and language of distress is constantly shifting. What matters here is how the person whose experience we are trying to understand names, describes, and makes sense of their experience. This is in line with hermeneutic phenomenology's aim to turn to the nature of the lived experience itself.

Chapter 5 The lived experience of navigating higher education with a mental health difficulty

1. Level 4 refers to a level on the National Framework of Qualifications. The framework consists of 10 levels. Level 4 aligns with a basic Leaving Certificate, or school leaving examination, while level 8 represents an honours bachelor's degree, level 9 a master's degree and level 10 a doctoral degree. Students typically progress from one level to the next in this framework.

References

Abdellah, F. and Levine, E. (1979) *Better Patient Care Through Nursing Research*. New York, NY: Macmillan Publishing.

Access College (2024) *What is DARE?* Dublin: Access College. Available at: https://accesscollege.ie/dare/what-is-dare/.

AHEAD (2012) *Survey on the Participation of Students with Disabilities in Higher Education for the Academic Year 2011/2012*. Dublin: AHEAD.

AHEAD (2016). *Mental Health Matters: Mapping Best Practices in Higher Education*. Dublin: Association for Higher Education Access and Disability.

AHEAD (2023). *Students with Disabilities Engaged with Support Services in Higher Education in Ireland 2021/22*. Dublin: AHEAD.

Al-Azawei, A., Serenelli, F. and Lundqvist, K. (2016). Universal Design for Learning (UDL): A Content Analysis of Peer-Reviewed Journal Papers from 2012 to 2015. *The Journal of Scholarship of Teaching and Learning*, 16(3), pp. 39–56.

Almeqdad, Q. I., Alodat, A. M., Alquraan, M. F., Mohaidat, M. A. and Al-Makhzoomy, A. K. (2023). The Effectiveness of Universal Design for Learning: A Systematic Review of the Literature and Meta-analysis. *Cogent Education*, 10(1).

Armstrong, N. and Byrom, N. C. (2023). The Impact of Mitigating Circumstances Procedures: Student Satisfaction, Wellbeing and Structural Compassion on the Campus. *Education Sciences*, 13(12), 1230.

Ashby, J. S. and Rice, K. G. (2002). Perfectionism, Dysfunctional Attitudes, and Self-Esteem: A Structural Equations Analysis. *Journal of Counseling and Development*, 80(2), pp. 197–203.

Australian Government Department of Home Affairs (2021). *Immigration and Citizenship: Meeting Our Requirements*. Australia: Australian Government Department of Home Affairs. Available at: https://immi.homeaffairs.gov.au/help-support/meeting-our-requirements/health.

Barker, P., Campbell, P. and Davidson, B. (1999). Introduction. In: P. Barker, P. Campbell and B. Davidson, eds., *From the Ashes of Experiences: Reflections on Madness, Survival and Growth*. London: Whurr Publishers.

Barthes, R. (1986). *The Rustle of Language*. New York: Hill and Wang.

Bateson, G. (1972). *Steps to an Ecology of Mind*. New York: Ballantine.

Beauchamp, T. L. and Childress, J. F. (2001). *Principles of Biomedical Ethics*. New York: Oxford University Press.

Belkin, D., Levitz, J. and Korn, M. (2019). Many More Students, Especially the Affluent, Get Extra Time to Take the SAT. *Wall Street Journal*.

Benner, P. (1994). The tradition and skill of interpretive phenomenology in studying health, illness and caring practices. In: P. Benner, ed., *Interpretive Phenomenology: Embodiment, Caring and Ethics in Health and Illness*. Thousand Oaks CA: Sage.

Beresford, P. (2005). "Service User": Regressive or Liberatory Terminology? *Disability & Society,* 20(4), pp. 469–477.

Bernstein, R. (1991). *The New Constellation: The Ethical-Political Horizons of Modernity/Postmodernity*. Cambridge: Polity Press.

Block, V. J., Haller, E., Villanueva, J., Meyer, A., Benoy, C., Walter, M., Lang, U. E. and Gloster, A. T. (2022). Meaningful Relationships in Community and Clinical Samples: Their Importance for Mental Health. *Frontiers in Psychology.*, 13, 832520.

Boss, M. (1979). *Existential Foundations of Medicine and Psychology*. New York: Aronson.

Bracken, P. (2015). Transforming Psychiatry: From Reductionism to Hermeneutics. *IIMHN*, Trinity College Dublin School of Nursing, 5 June.

Bracken, P. and Thomas, P. (2001). Post Psychiatry: A New Direction for Mental Health. *British Medical Journal*, 322, pp. 724–727.

Bracken, P. and Thomas, P. (2005). *Postpsychiatry: Mental Health in a Postmodern World*. Oxford: Oxford University Press.

Bracken, P., Thomas, P., Timimi, S., Asen, E., Behr, G., Beuster, C., Bhunnoo, S., Browne, I., Chhina, N., Double, D., Downer, S., Evans, C., Fernando, S., Garland, M., Hopkins, W., Huws, R., Johnson, B., Martindale, B., Middleton, H., Moldavsky, D., Moncrieff, J., Mullins, S., Nelki, J., Pizzo, M., Rodger, J., Smyth, M., Summerfield, D., Wallace, J. and Yeomans, D. (2012). Psychiatry Beyond the Current Paradigm. *The British Journal of Psychiatry*, 201, pp. 430–434.

Braun, V. and Clarke, V. (2006). Using Thematic Analysis in Psychology. *Qualitative Research in Psychology*, 3(2), pp. 77–101.

Brown, B. (2015). *Daring Greatly: How the Courage to be Vulnerable Transforms the Way We Live, Love, Parent and Lead*. New York: Avery Publishing.

Burns, T. (2006). *Psychiatry: A Very Short Introduction*. Oxford: Oxford University Press.

Campbell, J., Davidson, G., Kirwan, G., McCartan, C. and McFadden, D. (2022). The Mental Health Needs of Social Work Students: Findings from an Irish Survey. *Social Work Education*, ahead-of-print, pp. 1–17.

Capp, M. J. (2017). The Effectiveness of Universal Design for Learning: A Meta-analysis of Literature between 2013 and 2016. *International Journal of Inclusive Education*, 21(8), pp. 791–807.

Caspi, A., Houts, R. M., Ambler, A., Danese, A., Elliott, M. L., Hariri, A., Harrington, H., Hogan, S., Poulton, R., Ramrakha, S., Rasmussen, L. J. H., Reuben, A., Richmond-Rakerd, L., Sugden, K., Wertz, J.,

Williams, B. S. and Moffitt, T. E. (2020). Longitudinal Assessment of Mental Health Disorders and Comorbidities Across 4 Decades Among Participants in the Dunedin Birth Cohort Study. *JAMA Network Open*, 3(4), pp. e203221–e203221.

Central Applications Office (2024). *Points Calculator*. Dublin: Central Statistics Office. Available at: www.cao.ie/index.php?page=points_calc (Accessed 29 February 2024).

Central Statistics Office (2000). *That Was Then, This Is Now. Change in Ireland, 1949–1999*. Dublin: Central Statistics Office.

Central Statistics Office (2016). Highest Level of Education Attained. Available at: www.cso.ie/en/releasesandpublications/hubs/p-opi/olderpersonsinformationhub/education/highestlevelofeducationattained/ (Accessed 12 January 2024).

Chesters, J., Smith, J., Hernan, C., Jacqueline, L.-B., Johanna, W., Zlatko, S. and Woodman, D. (2019). Young Adulthood in Uncertain Times: The Association Between Sense of Personal Control and Employment, Education, Personal Relationships and Health. *Journal of Sociology (Melbourne, Vic.)*, 55(2), pp. 389–408.

Citizens Information (2023). *Third Level Student Fees and Charges*. Dublin: Citizens Information. Available at: www.citizensinformation.ie/en/education/third-level-education/fees-and-supports-for-third-level-education/fees/#:~:text=The%20maximum%20rate%20of%20the,exemption%20from%20the%20student%20contribution. (Accessed 12 January 2024).

Claeys-Kulik, A., Jørgensen, T. and Stöber, H. (2019). *Diversity, Equity and Inclusion in European Higher Education Institutions Results from the INVITED Project*. Brussels: European Universities Association. Available at: https://eua.eu/downloads/publications/web_diversity%20equity%20and%20inclusion%20in%20european%20higher%20education%20institutions.pdf. (Accessed 25 July 2024).

Clancy, P. (1996). Pathways to Mass Higher Education in the Republic of Ireland. *European Journal of Education*, 31(3), pp. 355–370.

Coffey, A. and Atkinson, P. (1996). *Making Sense of Qualitative Data*. Thousand Oaks, CA: Sage.

Colley, H. (2007). Understanding Time in Learning Transitions through the Lifecourse. *International Studies in Sociology of Education*, 17(4), pp. 427–443.

Coppock, V. and Hopton, J. (2000). *Critical Perspectives on Mental Health*. London: Routledge.

Crichton, P., Carel, H. and Kidd, I. J. (2017). Epistemic Injustice in Psychiatry. *BJPsych Bull*, 41(2), pp. 65–70.

Cromby, J., Harper, D. and Reavey, P. (2013). *Psychology, Mental Health and Distress*. London: Palgrave.

Davies, J. (2021). *Sedated: How Modern Capitalism Created our Mental Health Crisis*. London: Atlantic Books.

Denzin, N. and Lincoln, Y. (2011). *Handbook of Qualitative Research*. 4th ed. Thousand Oaks, CA: Sage.

Department of Health (2020). *Sharing the Vision: A Mental Health Policy for Everyone*. Dublin: Department of Health.

Department of Health and Children (1984). *The Psychiatric Services: Planning for the Future*. Dublin: The Stationery Office.

Department of Health and Children (2006). *A Vision for Change*. Dublin: The Stationery Office.

Deutsch, A. (1937). *The Mentally Ill in America: A History of their Care and Treatment from Colonial Times*. New York: Columbia University Press.

Dillon, J. (2011). Recovery from "Psychosis". In: J. Geekie, P. Randal, D. Lampshire and J. Read, eds., *Experiencing Psychosis: Personal and Professional Perspectives*. Oxfordshire: Taylor & Francis Group.

Dillon, J. and Hornstein, G. (2013). Hearing Voices Peer Support Groups: A Powerful Alternative for People in Distress. *Psychosis*, 5(3), pp. 286–295.

Dooley, B. and Fitzgerald, A. (2012). *The My World Survey: National Study of Youth Mental Health in Ireland.* Dublin: Headstrong The National Centre for Youth Mental Health.

Dooley, B., O'Connor, C., Fitzgerald, A. and O'Reilly, A. (2019). *My World Survey 2: The National Study of Youth Mental Health in Ireland.* Dublin, Ireland: UCD and Jigsaw.

Ecclestone, K., Biesta, G. and Hughes, M., eds. (2010). *Transitions and Learning through the Lifecourse,* London: Routledge.

Eurostat (2022). *Disability: Higher Risk of Poverty or Social Exclusion.* Brussels: Eurostat.

Farrell, E. (2020). Researching Lived Experience in Education: Misunderstood or Missed Opportunity? *International Journal of Qualitative Methods*, 19.

Farrell, E. (2022a). Darkness, wellness and world views: the university's role in shaping students' experiences of mental health and distress. In: Á. Mahon, ed., *The Promise of the University: Reclaiming, Humanity, Humility and Hope*, pp. 133–143. Singapore: Springer.

Farrell, E. (2022b). *Making Sense of Mental Health: A Practical Approach Through Lived Experience.* Dublin: The Liffey Press.

Farrell, E. and Mahon, Á. (2021). Understanding Student Mental Health: Difficulty, Deflection and Darkness. *Ethics and Education*, 16(1), pp. 36–50.

Fava, N. and Baker, D. (2022). *Changing It Up: Supporting Young People to Navigate Life Transitions*. Melbourne: Orygen.

Felitti, V. J., Anda, R. F., Nordenberg, D., Williamson, D. F., Spitz, A. M., Edwards, V., Koss, M. P. and Marks, J. S. (1998). Relationship of Childhood Abuse and Household Dysfunction to Many of the Leading Causes of Death in Adults: The Adverse Childhood Experiences (ACE) Study. *American Journal of Preventive Medicine*, 14(4), pp. 245–258.

Finnane, M. (1981). *Insanity and the Insane in Post-famine Ireland*. London: Croom Helm.

Foucault, M. (1961). *Folie et déraison: Histoire de la folie à l'âge classique*. Paris: Plon.

Foucault, M. (2001). *Madness and Civilisation*. London: Routledge.

Foucault, M. (2006). *History of Madness*. London: Routledge.

Foulkes, L. (2021). *Losing Our Minds: What Mental Illness Really Is and What It Isn't*. London: The Bodley Head.

Frost, R. O., Marten, P., Lahart, C. and Rosenblate, R. (1990). The Dimensions of Perfectionism. *Cognitive Therapy and Research*, 14(5), pp. 449–468.

Gadamer, H. G. (1960/1989). *Truth and Method*. 2nd ed. London: Sheed and Ward.

Gadamer, H. G. (1979). *Truth and Method*. Translated by W. Glen-Doepel, 1st ed. London: Sheed & Ward.

Ginn, S. and Horder, J. (2012). "One in four" with a Mental Health Problem: The Anatomy of a Statistic. *BMJ*, 344(7845), pp. 31–e1302.

Goffman, E. (1961). *Asylums: Essays on the Social Situation of Mental Patients and Other Inmates*. New York: Anchor Books.

Goffman, E. (1963). *Stigma: Notes on the Social Management of a Spoiled Identity*. Englewood Cliffs, NJ: Prentice-Hall.

Goldberg, M., Hadas-Lidor, N. and Karnieli-Miller, O. (2015). From Patient to Therapatient: Social Work Students Coping with Mental Illness. *Qualitative Health Research*, 25(7), pp. 887–898.

Griesenger, W. (1867). Editorial. *Archives of Psychiatry and Nervous Disease*, 1.

Guba, E. (1990). The alternative paradigm dialogue. In: E. Guba, ed., *The Paradigm Dialogue*. Newbury Park, CA: Sage.

Harman, G. (2007). *Heidegger Explained: From Phenomenon to Thing*. Illinois: Open Court.

Healy, R., Banks, J. and Ryder, D. (2023). Universal design for learning policy in tertiary education in Ireland: Are we ready to commit? In: J. W. Madaus and L. L. Dukes, eds., *Handbook of Higher Education and Disability*. Cheltenham: Edward Elgar Publishing.

Heidegger, M. (1927/1996). *Being and Time*. New York: State University of New York Press.

Higgins, M. D. (2021). "On Academic Freedom" – Address at the Scholars at Risk Ireland/All European Academies Conference. *Scholars at Risk Ireland/All European Academies Conference*, Online. Available at: https://president.ie/en/media-library/speeches/on-academic-freedom-address-at-the-scholars-at-risk-ireland-all-european-academies-conference. (Accessed 25 July 2024).

Higher Education Authority (2020). *Higher Education Healthy Campus Charter & Framework for Ireland 2020–2025*. Dublin: Higher Education Authority. Available at: https://hea.ie/assets/uploads/2023/03/Healthy-Campus-Charter-and-Framework.pdf. (Accessed 25 July 2024).

Higher Education Authority (2023). *Fund for Students with Disabilities: Guidelines for Higher Education Institutions*. Dublin: Higher Education Authority.

Higher Education Authority (2024a). Deprivation Index Scores by Entry Basis of New Entrants. Available at: https://hea.ie/statistics/data-for-download-and-visualisations/students/widening-participation-for-equity-of-access/dis-2020/2-student-dis-2020/. (Accessed 25 July 2024).

Higher Education Authority (2024b). *Free Fees Initiative*. Dublin: Higher Education Authority. Available at: https://hea.ie/funding-governance-performance/funding/student-finance/course-fees/ (Accessed 29 February 2024).

Higher Education Authority (2024c). *Non-Progression Rates of New Entrants 2021/2022 (Year 1, Full-time Undergraduate)*.

Dublin: Higher Education Authority. Available at: https://hea.ie/statistics/data-for-download-and-visualisations/students/progression-and-completion-dashboard/ (Accessed 29 February 2024).

Hornstein, G. (2017). *Agnes's Jacket: A Psychologist's Search for the Meanings of Madness*. London: Routledge.

Horowitz, A., ed. (2020). *Between Sanity and Madness: Mental Illness from Ancient Greece to the Neuroscientific Era*. Oxford: Oxford University Press.

Houses of the Oireachtas (2023). *Joint Committee on Education, Further and Higher Education, Research, Innovation and Science. The Future of Science, Technology, Engineering and Maths (STEM) in Irish Education*. Dublin: Houses of the Oireachtas. Available at: https://opac.oireachtas.ie/Data/Library3/Documents%20Laid/2023/pdf/153doclaid170723_164033.pdf.

Hutchison, E. D. (2008). *Dimensions of Human Behavior: The Changing Life Course*. SAGE Publications.

Inspectors of Lunatics (1901). *The Fiftieth Report of the Inspectors of Lunatics (Ireland)*. Dublin.

Inspectors of Lunatics (1906). *The Fifty-Fourth Report of the Inspectors of Lunatics (Ireland)*. Dublin.

Institute of Public Administration (2024). *Ireland: A Directory*. Dublin: Institute of Public Administration.

Irish Universities Association (2023). *Investing in Skills & Talent and the Capacity of Universities to Support Core National Priorities*. Dublin: Irish Universities Association. Available at: www.iua.ie/wp-content/uploads/2023/10/19.9.23-Letter_Taoiseach_Ministers_IUA_Universities.pdf.

Jensen, M. and Redman, L. (2024). Response to "The Importance of Diversity in Obesity Articles". *Obesity*, 32(3), 444 *(Silver Spring, Md.)*.

Johnstone, L. (2000). *Users and Abusers of Psychiatry: A Critical Look at Psychiatric Practice*. London: Routledge.

Johnstone, L., Boyle, M., Cromby, J., Dillon, J., Harper, D., Kinderman, P., Longden, E., Pilgrim, D. and Read, J. (2018). *The Power Threat Meaning Framework*. Leicester: British Psychological Society.

Kayis, A. R. and Ceyhan, A. A. (2015). Investigating the Achievement Goals of University Students in Terms of Psycho-social Variables. *Educational Sciences: Theory & Practice*, 15(2), 445.

Kelly, B. (2016). *Hearing Voices: The History of Psychiatry in Ireland*. Co. Kildare: Irish Academic Press.

Kelly, B. (2023). *Asylum: Inside Grangegorman*. Dublin: Royal Irish Academy.

Kelly, F. (2005). *A Guide to Early Irish Law*. Dublin: Dublin Institute for Advanced Studies.

Kessler, R., Berglund, P., Demler, O., Jin, R., Merikangas, K. R. and Walters, E. E. (2005). Lifetime Prevalence and Age-of-Onset Distributions of DSM-IV Disorders in the National Comorbidity Survey Replication. *Archives of General Psychiatry*, 62(6), pp. 593–602.

Kirkpatrick, T. P. (1931). *A Note on the History of the Care of the Insane in Ireland up to the End of the Nineteenth Century*. Dublin: Dublin University Press.

Kleinman, A. (1991). *Rethinking Psychiatry: From Cultural Category to Personal Experience*. New York: Free Press.

Kleinman, A. (2012). Rebalancing Academic Psychiatry: Why It Needs to Happen – and Soon. *The British Journal of Psychiatry*, 201, pp. 421–422.

Koch, T. (1994). Establishing Rigour in Qualitative Research: The Decision Trail. *Journal of Advanced Nursing*, 19(5), pp. 976–986.

Krause, K.-L. (2005). Serious Thoughts about Dropping Out in First Year: Trends, Patterns and Implications for Higher Education. *Studies in Learning, Evaluation, Innovation and Development*, 2(3), pp. 55–68.

Laing, R. D. (1960). *The Divided Self.* London: Penguin.

Lincoln, Y. and Guba, E. (1985). Postpositivism and the Naturalistic Paradigm. In: Y. Lincoln and E. Guba, eds., *Naturalistic Inquiry*. London: Sage.

Lunn, J., Greene, D., Callaghan, T. and Egan, S. J. (2023). Associations Between Perfectionism and Symptoms of Anxiety, Obsessive-Compulsive Disorder and Depression in Young People: A Meta-analysis. *Cognitive Behaviour Therapy*, 52(5), pp. 460–487.

Maguire, M. (2023). "It has stunted my life": Readers Share Their Experiences of Adults Living with Their Parents. *Journal.ie*, 5 September.

Mahon, A. (2021). *The Promise of the University: Reclaiming Humanity, Humility, and Hope.* 1st ed. Gateway East, Singapore: Springer.

Manthorpe, J. and Stanley, N. (1999). Dilemmas in Professional Education: Responding Effectively to Students with Mental Health Problems. *Journal of Interprofessional Care*, 13(4), 355.

Marcel, G. (1950). *Mystery of Being.* South Bend, Indiana: Gateway Editions.

Maté, G. and Maté, D. (2022). *The Myth of Normal: Trauma, Illness & Healing in a Toxic Culture.* London: Vermilion.

McCarthy, P., Quirke, M. and Treanor, D. (2018). *The Role of the Disability Officer and the Disability Service in Higher Education in Ireland.* Dublin: AHEAD Educational Press. Available at: www.ahead.ie/userfiles/files/shop/free/The%20_Role_of_the_Disability_Officer.pdf.

McInerney, S. (2021). Refused Mortgage Protection due to Mental Illness. 5 August. Radio interview "Drive Time" RTE Radio 1.

Mind (2022). *Life Insurance and Mental Health.* London: Mind. Available at: www.mind.org.uk/media/12190/insurance-2022-pdf-for-download-pdf-version.pdf. (Accessed 25 July 2024).

Ministry of Defence (2018). *JSP 950 Medical Policy: Joint Service Manual of Medical Fitness*. London: Ministry of Defence. Available at: https://data.parliament.uk/DepositedPapers/Files/DEP2019-0604/Joint_Service_Manual_of_Medical_Fitness.pdf. (Accessed 25 July 2024).

Moncrieff, J. (2007). *The Myth of the Chemical Cure: A Critique of Psychiatric Drug Treatment*. London: Palgrave Macmillan.

Moncrieff, J. (2013). *The Bitterest Pills: The Troubling Story of Antipsychotic Drugs*. London: Palgrave Macmillan.

Morel, B. A. (1857). *Traité des dégénérescences physiques, intellectuelles et morales de l'espèce humaine et des causes qui produisent ces variétés maladives*. Paris: J. B. Baillière.

Munhall, P. (1994). *Revisioning Phenomenology Nursing and Health Science Research*. New York: National League for Nursing Press.

Munhall, P. (2012). *Nursing Research: A Qualitative Perspective*. 5th ed. Sudbury, MA: Jones and Bartlett.

Newman, J. H. (2009). *The Idea of a University*. 2nd ed. Dublin: UCD International Centre for Newman Studies.

O'Brien, C. (2023). Why Are College Dropout Rates on the Up in Ireland? *The Irish Times*, 27 September. Available at: https://www.irishtimes.com/ireland/education/2023/09/27/why-are-college-dropout-rates-on-the-up/. (Accessed 25 July 2024).

O'Brien, C. (2024). "A perfect storm": Why More Students Are Dropping Out of College. *The Irish Times*. Available at: www.irishtimes.com/ireland/education/2024/02/29/a-perfect-storm-why-more-students-are-dropping-out-of-college/. (Accessed 25 July 2024).

Oakeshott, M. (1989). The Idea of a University. In: T. Fuller, ed., *The Voice of Liberal Learning: Michael Oakeshott on Education*, pp. 23–30. New Haven, CT: Yale University Press.

Oreskes, N. (2021). *Why Trust Science?* New Jersey: Princeton University Press.

Padden, L. and Tonge, J. (2018). A Review of the Disability Access Route to Education in UCD 2010–2013. *International Journal of Disability, Development, and Education*, 65(1), pp. 90–107.

Parker, P. D., Ciarrochi, J., Heaven, P., Marshall, S., Sahdra, B. and Kiuru, N. (2015). Hope, Friends, and Subjective Well-Being: A Social Network Approach to Peer Group Contextual Effects. *Child Development*, 86(2), pp. 642–650.

Pointon-Haas, J., Waqar, L., Upsher, R., Foster, J., Byrom, N. and Oates, J. (2023). A Systematic Review of Peer Support Interventions for Student Mental Health and Well-being in Higher Education. *BJPsych Open*, 10(1), pp. e12–e12.

Polit, D. F. and Hungler, B. P. (1999). *Nursing Research: Principles and Methods*. 6th ed. Philadelphia: Lippincott Williams and Wilkins.

Polkinghorne, D. (2007). Validity Issues in Narrative Research. *Qualitative Inquiry*, 13(4), pp. 471–486.

Productivity Commission (2020). *Mental Health, Inquiry Report No. 95*. Canberra: Australian Government Productivity Commission.

Psychological Society of Ireland (2011). *Code of Professional Ethics*. Dublin: Psychological Society of Ireland.

Quinn, J. (2009). Rethinking "failed transitions" to Higher Education. In K. Ecclestone, G. Biesta, and M. Hughes, eds. *Transitions and Learning through the Lifecourse*, pp. 118–129. London: Routledge.

Quinn Patton, M. (2002). *Qualitative Research and Evaluation Methods*. 3rd ed. Newbury Park: Sage.

Quirke, M., Mc Guckin, C. and McCarthy, P. (2023). *Adopting a UDL Attitude Within Academia: Understanding and Practicing Inclusion across Higher Education*. 1st ed. Milton: Routledge.

Raftery, D. (2011). "Among School Children": The Churches, Politics and Irish Schooling, 1830–1930. *Studies (Dublin)*, 100(400), pp. 433–440.

Rainbow, P. and Sullivan, W. (1987). *The Interpretive Turn: A Second Look*. Berkeley, CA: California Press.

ReachOut Australia (2022). New Research Finds that Stress About the Future Is Impacting the Wellbeing of Young Aussies. Available at: https://about.au.reachout.com/blog/new-research-finds-that-stress-about-the-future-is-impacting-the-wellbeing-of-young-aussies.

Roberts, K. and Taylor, B. (1998). *Nursing Research Processes: An Australian Perspective*. South Melbourne, Australia: Nelson ITP.

Robins, J. (1986). *Fools and Mad: A History of the Insane in Ireland*. Dublin: Institute of Public Administration.

Rogers, A. and Pilgrim, D. (2014). *A Sociology of Mental Health and Illness*. 4th ed. Berkshire, UK: Open University Press.

Rorty, R. (1979). *Philosophy and the Mirror of Nature*. Princeton, NJ: Princeton University Press.

Rose, D. (2017). Service User/Survivor-led Research in Mental Health: Epistemological Possibilities. *Disability & Society*, 32(6), pp. 773–789.

Rose, N. (1998). *Inventing Our Selves: Psychology, Power and Personhood*. Cambridge: Cambridge University Press.

Rose, N. (2006). Disorders Without Borders? The Expanding Scope of Psychiatric Practice. *BioSocieties*, 1(4), pp. 465–484.

Rose, N. (2019). *Our Psychiatric Future*. Cambridge: Polity.

Rose, P. (1985). *Writing on Women: Essays in a Renaissance*. Middletown, CT: Wesleyan University Press.

Sandelowski, M. (1986). The Problem of Rigor in Qualitative Research. *Advances in Nursing Science*, 8(3), 11.

Scull, A. (1979). *Museums of Madness: The Social Organisation of Insanity in Nineteenth Century England.* London: Penguin.

Scull, A. (2011). *Madness: A Very Short Introduction.* Oxford: Oxford University Press.

Semple, D. and Smyth, R. (2013). *Oxford Handbook of Psychiatry.* 3rd ed. Oxford: Oxford University Press.

Sharp, E., Wray, R. and Maxwell, R. (2020). Improving Student Retention through Enhanced Academic and Pastoral Support: A Case Study. *Innovative Practice in Higher Education*, 4(1), pp. 39–56.

Soek, S., DaCosta, B. and Hodges, R. (2018). A Systematic Review of Empirically Based Universal Design for Learning: Implementation and Effectiveness of Universal Design in Education for Students With and Without Disabilities at the Postsecondary Level. *Open Journal of Social Sciences*, 6.

Spiegelberg, H. (1984). Three Types of the Given: The Encountered, the Search-found and the Striking. *Husserl Studies*, 1, pp. 69–78.

Stanley, N., Ridley, J., Harris, J. and Manthorpe, J. (2011). Disclosing Disability in the Context of Professional Regulation: A Qualitative UK Study. *Disability & Society*, 26(1), pp. 19–32.

Steeves, R. (2000). Sampling. *Hermeneutic Phenomenological Research: A Practical Guide for Nurse Researchers.* Thousand Oaks, CA: Sage.

Stoeber, J., Haskew, A. E. and Scott, C. (2015). Perfectionism and Exam Performance: The Mediating Effect of Task-approach Goals. *Personality and Individual Differences*, 74, pp. 171–176.

Stoeber, J. and Otto, K. (2006). Positive Conceptions of Perfectionism: Approaches, Evidence, Challenges. *Personality and Social Psychology Review*, 10(4), pp. 295–319.

Szasz, T. (1960). The Myth of Mental Illness. *American Psychologist*, 15, pp. 113–118.

Szasz, T. (1961). *Myth of Mental Illness*. New York: Harper & Row.

The Guardian (2023). The Guardian View on Universities: Arts Cuts Are the Tip of the Iceberg. *The Guardian*, 26 June. Available at: www.theguardian.com/commentisfree/2023/jun/26/the-guardian-view-on-universities-arts-cuts-are-the-tip-of-an-iceberg#:~:text=In%20cutting%20the%20arts%20and,1992%20universities%20should%20be%20junked.

The Irish Times (2023). Irish Times Feeder Schools 2023. *The Irish Times*. Available at: www.irishtimes.com/ireland/education/2023/12/12/feeder-schools-school-leavers-from-disadvantaged-areas-progress-to-college-in-near-record-numbers/#:~:text=Overall%2C%20this%20year%27s%20data%20shows,to%20third%20level%20in%202023. (Accessed 25th July 2024)

Timmis, M. A., Pexton, S. and Cavallerio, F. (2022). Student Transition into Higher Education: Time for a Rethink within the Subject of Sport and Exercise Science? *Frontiers in Education (Lausanne)*, 7.

US Department of Health and Human Services (2001). *Mental Health: Culture, Race, and Ethnicity—A Supplement to Mental Health: A Report of the Surgeon General*. Rockville, Maryland: US Department of Health and Human Services,.

Van der Kolk, B. A. (2014). *The Body Keeps the Score: Mind, Brain and Body in the Transformation of Trauma*. London: Penguin Books.

Van Manen, M. (1990). *Researching Lived Experience: Human Science for an Action Sensitive Pedagogy*. New York: State University of New York Press.

Walsh, D. and Daly, A. (2004). *Mental Illness in Ireland 1750–2002: Reflections on the Rise and Fall of Institutional Care*. Dublin: Health Research Board.

Watson, J. (2019). *Drop the Disorder! Challenging the Culture of Psychiatric Diagnosis*. Manchester: PCCS Books.

Watts, J. (2017). Is Mental Illness Real?, *The Guardian*, 12 April. www.theguardian.com/commentisfree/2017/apr/12/is-mental-illness-real-google-answer.

Watts, M. (2012). *Recovery from "mental illness" as a re-enchantment with life: a narrative study*. Ph.D. University of Dublin, Dublin.

Winn, S. (2002). Student Motivation: A Socio-economic Perspective. *Studies in Higher Education (Dorchester-on-Thames)*, 27(4), pp. 445–457.

Wolcott, H. (1994). *Transforming Qualitative Data*. Thousand Oaks, CA: Sage Publications.

Zając, T., Perales, F., Tomaszewski, W., Xiang, N. and Zubrick, S. R. (2024). Student Mental Health and Dropout from Higher Education: An Analysis of Australian Administrative Data. *Higher Education*, 87(2), pp. 325–343.

Index

adverse childhood experiences. 15
Alzheimer, Alois. 14
anorexia nervosa. 62
anticipatory stress. 27

Bateson, G. 101
Beauchamp. 129
beneficence. 130
Benner, P. 101
Bernstein, R. 110
brain anomalies. 14
Braun, V. 115, 116, 118
Brehon Laws. 11
British National Centre for Research Methods. 107
Brown, B. 80

Cartesian Dualism. 19
Central Applications Office (CAO). 34, 35
Childers. 129
Clarke, V. 115, 116, 118
Clinical Placement Co-ordinator (CPC). 50

Colley, H. 26
confidentiality. 128, 129
confirmability. 122, 126, 127
conventionalists. 121
conversational interviewing. 110, 127
COVID-19 pandemic. 29
credibility. 122, 124
crippling anxiety. 61

Declaration of Helsinki. 128
degeneration. 13
Department of Further and Higher Education, Research, Innovation and Science (DFHERIS). 8
dependability. 122, 125, 127
Disability Access Route to Education (DARE) scheme. 20, 26, 33, 34, 35, 36, 37, 90
disability support; diagnosis. 40, 42; disability support service. 42, 43, 45; mental health difficulty. 45, 46, 49, 50, 51, 52; psychiatric diagnosis. 40
discrimination. 15

distress. 3, 131; and mental health. 6; biological basis. 7, 14; diagnosis. 40, 42, 52, 80; FSD. 18; illness framework, or biomedical model. 15; in higher education. 64, 97; language related. 6; lived experience. 4, 5, 107; medico-scientific approach. 5; psychological. 128, 130, 131; students experience. 45, 47, 56, 86, 88, 93, 97; transition to higher education. 26

dyslexia. 75

electricity-induced seizures. 14

ethical considerations. 127; beneficence. 130, 131; confidentiality. 128, 129; informed consent. 128; justice. 131; non-maleficence. 131; respect for autonomy. 129

"fitness to practice" standards. 46

Free Fees Initiative. 17, 29, 91

free second level education. 91

Fund for Students with Disabilities (FSD). 18, 40, 42

Gadamer, H. G. 100, 115

generalisability. 105, 124

Guba, E. 121, 125, 126

Heidegger. 96, 99, 101, 103, 115

hermeneutic phenomenological method. 98, 99; data generation. 111, 112, 113, 114, 115; method. 104; paradigm. 101, 102, 103; research questions. 105; sample size. 107, 108; sampling. 106, 107

hermeneutic phenomenology. 7

Higgins, Michael D. 94

Higher Education Authority (HEA). 8, 16, 21

Higher Education Institutions (HEIs). 8, 34

higher education, transition to; "the gift of an interval". 27; challenges and opportunities. 29; description. 26; distress. 25; experience of transition. 30, 31, 32, 33; mismatched expectations or anticipatory stress. 27; with mental health difficulties. 28

Houses of Industry, Dublin. 12

human difficulty. *see* distress

inequity. 15

informed consent. 128

insulin-induced comas. 14

Ireland; arrival of Christianity. 10; higher education. 9; DARE scheme. 20, 21; Free Fees Initiative. 17; history of. 16; scarce resources. 17; state-funded primary and secondary education. 16; with mental health difficulties. 18, 19; housing crisis. 29; Law of

Distress. 11; mental health. 10, 12, 13, 14, 15

Irish druids. 10

justice. 131

Kelly, Brendan. 14

Koch, T. 124

Leaving Certificate examination. 35, 62, 71, 98

Lincoln, Y. 122, 125, 126

lived experience, with mental health difficulties. 56; at university. 65, 66, 68, 69; higher education for students; challenges. 56, 64; depression and anxiety. 59, 60; National Framework of Qualifications. 62, 63, 98; navigating higher education. 57, 58; poverty and abuse. 60, 61; with distress. 64; perfectionism. 69, 71, 73, 75, 76, 77, 79, 80

malarial mosquitoes. 14

medical microbiology. 13

mental distress. *see* distress

mental health difficulties. 8; at university. 65, 67, 68, 69; higher education for students. 56, 58, 59, 60, 61, 62, 63, 64; lived experience. 3, 5; support for students. 89, 90

mental health policy, Ireland. 7

mental health problem or mental health condition. 7

mental illness. 6, 7, 8, 14, 15, 51, 58, 64, 68, 82

mismatched expectations. 27

missed opportunities. 28

"mitigating circumstances", ethnographic study of. 21

Munhall, P. 103

National Centre for Youth Mental Health, Ireland. 4

National Framework of Qualifications. 98

Newman, John Henry. 95

non-maleficence. 131

non-probability sampling. 106

occupational health. 50

Oxford Handbook of Psychiatry. 15

panic attacks. 61

pathology. 7

Patton, Quinn. 107

perfectionism. 69, 71, 73, 75, 76, 77, 79, 80

phenomenological methods; data analysis. 115; hermeneutic circle. 116, 119, 120, 121

policy. 6, 7, 86, 96

Polkinghorne, D. 121

power. 15

prefrontal lobotomy. 14

procrastination. 77

"professional veneer". 46

psychiatry; active engagement. 5; defined. 13; development of. 13; explanation of mental disorder. 14; history of. 14; illness framework. 14

psychological distress. 128, 130, 131. *see also* distress

purposive sampling. 106

Quinn, J. 26

Rainbow, P. 103

reformists. 121

respect for autonomy. 130

Roberts, K. 114

Robins, J. 11

Science Technology Engineering and Mathematics (STEM). 95

Seanchas Mór, or "Law of Distress". 11

self-awareness. 81

social approval. 63

Social Darwinism. 13

student counselling services. 28

Sullivan, W. 102

syphilis-induced psychosis. 14

Taylor, B. 114

transferability. 122, 125

transition. *see also* higher education, transition to; defined. 26; experience of. 30

trauma. 15

trustworthiness. 121, 122, 123

universal design for learning (UDL) approach. 22, 90

university, transition to; celebrating and investing. 94, 95; experience and knowledge of students. 96; financing widening participation. 91, 92; investing in people and relationships. 92, 94; supporting transitions. 87, 89; with mental health difficulties. 89, 91

van Manen. 110

Weber, Max. 95

well-being. 10, 18

Wolcott, Harry. 106

www.ingramcontent.com/pod-product-compliance
Lightning Source LLC
Chambersburg PA
CBHW070808230426
43665CB00017B/2527